CULINARY
HISTORY *of the*
FINGER LAKES

CULINARY HISTORY *of the* FINGER LAKES

FROM THE THREE SISTERS TO RIESLING

LAURA WINTER FALK

AMERICAN PALATE

Published by American Palate
A Division of The History Press
Charleston, SC 29403
www.historypress.net

First published 2014
Second printing 2015

Manufactured in the United States

ISBN 978.1.62619.545.5

Library of Congress Cataloging-in-Publication Data

Falk, Laura Winter.
Culinary history of the Finger Lakes : from the Three Sisters to riesling / Laura Winter
Falk.
pages cm. -- (American palate)
ISBN 978-1-62619-545-5 (pbk.)
1. Food habits--New York (State)--Finger Lakes Region. 2. Food--Social aspects--New York
(State)--Finger Lakes Region. 3. Wine and wine making--New York (State)--Finger Lakes
Region. 4. Restaurants--New York (State)--Finger Lakes Region. I. Title.
GT2853.U5F36 2014
394.1'209747--dc23
2014035066

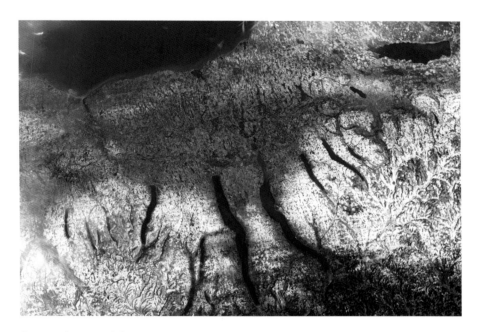

Courtesy of www.earthobservatory.nasa.gov.

The book is dedicated to my parents, Henrietta and Don Winter, who taught me to always embrace the opportunities and experiences that life brings.

CONTENTS

CONTENTS

PREFACE

In the words of Ulysses Prentiss Hendrick, "the author hopes that anyone who opens this book will take the time to read its brief preface," as it lays out the intention of the book so that the reader can decide whether he or she wants to read it. This book is a celebration of a region and its people. It weaves a story of the relationship between the two from the beginning of their coexistence to the present day and how it has evolved over time. It is not a comprehensive sourcebook of the complete history of Finger Lakes wine, agriculture or food. If you are looking for that, I suggest you peruse some of the wonderful books referenced in the bibliography, like Mr. Hendrick's. Instead, this book is intended to be more like a conversation people would have while sitting on the front porch of their farmhouse, drinking beers or wine on a warm summer's night—"Do you remember when…?" "So how did that get that way anyhow?" "Have you tasted the food or wine at…?"

The book is also intended to be a gift. Seven years ago, when my husband and I founded Experience! The Finger Lakes and set out to start a company that showed people "why those who live here stay here, and those who visit come back again and again," our goal was to show off the best that the region had to offer. We set out to provide our guests immersive experiences that create a relationship with the people and the region. Achieving this mission requires the forging of partnerships with businesses and artisans who 1) have amazing products and 2) understand the value of providing the best possible experiences. It means asking our partners to dedicate their valuable time and staff, often during the busiest times, to stop and visit with our guests and share their products, passions and stories. This book is not only a thank-you to them but also a gift to all the readers who now have the opportunity to get to know these businesses and artisans and the fabulous items they are creating. Then, perhaps, they will get inspired to come here and experience the Finger Lakes for themselves. In doing this, it is very important to note that there are hundreds of wonderful farms, wineries and other artisan beverage manufacturers, food producers, chefs and restaurants in this vast region doing incredible things. To try to include them all would go way beyond the purpose of this book. Instead, I tried to offer readers a metaphorical and literal taste of the region—an impressionistic painting intended to invite them to come and fill in the dots and details for themselves when they visit.

Lastly, pairing recipes with currently available Finger Lakes wines was a way to link the culinary past with the present. With each era, a chef was given the task of using specific ingredients or a type of recipe (or even re-creating an entire menu) to pay homage to the period he or she was representing. The exciting part was giving the chefs free reign to personalize and/or modernize the recipes so that they would be as exciting today as they were when they were first conceived. Pairing them with today's wines was truly the icing on the cake—my tip-of-the-hat to the timelessness of our local food and beverages, which are so seamlessly intertwined in defining our region and its culinary history.

ACKNOWLEDGEMENTS

Many acknowledgement sections in books start out by thanking the editor, "for without him/her, this book would not have been written." At risk of sounding cliché, I have to do it. I must start by thanking my editor, Whitney Landis, as were it not for her, this book truly would not have been written. Somehow, she identified me as someone who might have a story to tell about the Finger Lakes, and she trusted that it was a good one and that I had the skills to write it. What a leap of faith! I hope I created a book that validates the trust that she had in me from the start. She was incredibly patient and highly supportive during the entire process, and I am truly thankful for her and The History Press editorial board for buying into my vision and giving me this opportunity to share my love and passion for this region.

Much appreciation goes to Robyn Wishna, who photographed the amazing recipe and wine pairing images for this book. Robyn's talents in capturing the essence and beauty of the chef's creations are so apparent in every shot. Her love and appreciation for the local food scene in the Finger Lakes practically jump off the page when you look at her images. I am so proud and honored to have her as a significant contributor to this book, and I truly enjoyed working with her on this project.

To me, what makes this book so special is the contribution of my eight very busy and very talented chefs: Mary Jane Challen-Kircher, Samantha Buyskes, Brud Holland, Cookie Wheeler, Scott Signori, Wynnie Stein from Moosewood, Suzanne Stack and Emma Frisch. They were all so generous with their time and energy. They all embraced their assigned eras with excitement and enthusiasm and translated their passion for food and the Finger Lakes into their recipes and stories in the most beautiful way. I am lucky to know and have the opportunity to work with each of these special people. For this, I am truly grateful.

A big thank-you goes out to my winery partners: Cayuga Ridge Winery, Bet the Farm Winery, Sheldrake Point Winery, Hosmer Winery, Standing Stone Vineyards, Six Mile Creek Winery, Finger Lakes Distilling, Long Point Winery, Dr. Konstantin Frank Vinifera Wine Cellars, Red Newt Cellars, Silver Thread Vineyard, Damiani Wine Cellars, King Ferry Winery and Ports of New York. They graciously donated their wine for the photo shoots and the (oh so) important tasting necessary for the recipe and wine pairing section. I am honored to serve as an ambassador to their fantastic products, and I am inspired to tirelessly continue to promote the Finger Lakes wine region and all it represents.

I am grateful to the many organizations and people who generously provided the stunning images to help the culinary story of the region come alive on the pages of this book. In particular, there were those who allowed me to use a number of their images: Bill Hecht, Tony Ingraham, Laura Gallup, Andrew Noyes, Heron Hill Winery, the Ontario Visitor's Connection, the Ithaca Visitors and Convention Center and Dr. Konstantin Frank Vinifera Wine Cellars. A very special thank-you goes to the talented Christopher Loomis, who created elegant custom illustrations of the natural history and the Three Sisters for the introduction and first chapter.

I also must take a moment to thank Diana Campbell and Kristy Mitchell for taking the time out of their very busy lives to read through the book and provide me with their candid comments. Special recognition must go to Rebecca Long, my summer intern, who swept in like Super Woman and worked her magic in acquiring and organizing my images and formatting the manuscript so that both could be submitted to the publisher on time.

Writing a book does not happen in a vacuum, especially when you are running a business full time and raising a family. The only way it was possible for me to pull this off was due to the incredible work and support of Grace Scarpino-Stoutenburg, Experience! The Finger Lakes' touring coordinator. During the early stages of the book, Grace diligently worked her way through hundreds of websites, sent scores of e-mails and made numerous calls to start the collection of images for the book. Once the touring season picked up, she operated the office so efficiently that I was able to use all the precious minutes I needed to write the book. Without

Grace's support and hard work during these times, there would be no book, and for that I am so appreciative.

Lastly, any author can tell you that writing a book is kind of a self-absorbed activity that requires a lot of attention, focus and time. I am so lucky to have a family who was incredibly supportive during the writing of this book. My sons, Gabriel and Jackson, gave me the flexibility I needed to spend most weekends writing while laundry piled up and were always willing to listen to a paragraph here and there and give me their feedback. A mother could not ask for more special children in her life. Last, and most importantly, I give heartfelt thanks and appreciation to my husband and business partner, Alan Falk. Over twenty years ago, he agreed to take this journey through life with me. While my parents instilled in me the desire to reach for the stars, Alan has built a foundation of love, support and commitment that allows us to journey there together. He continues to encourage me to follow my dreams and passions even though there are many times when they dominate my time and energy. I am thankful to have him as my partner as we continue to make our life together in the Finger Lakes.

INTRODUCTION

There is something truly magical about New York's Finger Lakes region:
nine thousand square miles of deciduous rolling hills that put on an
autumn finale of luscious bounty and mind-blowing Technicolor each year.
It is home to eleven long, thin lakes of pristine blue that dramatically cut
through the hills, as if Grandma's cat was let loose on her favorite Turkish
rug. The formation of this landscape is a composite of over 300 million
years of evolution that has created a unique meso-climate that offers its
inhabitants an optimal environment in which to grow, live and thrive.

During the Devonian period, the Finger Lakes region was part of an
enormous inland sea that spanned thousands of square miles above what is
now Canada, over to Kentucky and down to North Carolina. During this
time, the continents were formed together in the supercontinent known as
Pangaea. The sea, and its position within the supercontinent, was very close
to the equator, making it tropical and brimming with life. Over millions of
years, as the depth of the sea would ebb and flow, it would leave layers of
deposits that would eventually form the region's characteristic landscape of
mineral-rich shale and limestone and create the basis of its *terroir* (*terroir* is
a French term that represents all the natural conditions in which food is
grown, including climate, soil and topography).

Flash-forward millions of years to the ice age, when enormous
glaciers—mile-deep forces of moving ice—existed in the region between
2 million and ten thousand years ago. These glaciers formed in the beds of
rivers that flowed into what we now call Lake Ontario. The glaciers would

Vineyards overlooking Keuka Lake. *Photo by Nicole Young, courtesy of Dr. Konstantin Frank Vinifera Wine Cellars.*

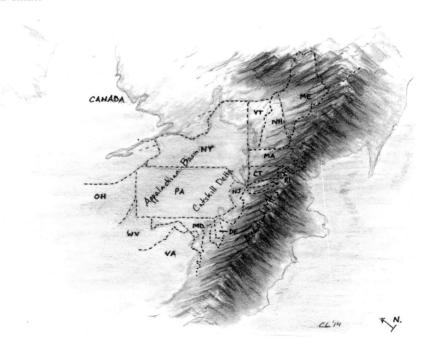

During the Devonian period, over 300 million years ago, erosion of the Acadian Mountains into the inland sea deposited the materials that became the sedimentary rock that today underlies the Finger Lakes region. *Illustration by Christopher Loomis (loomisart.wordpress.com).*

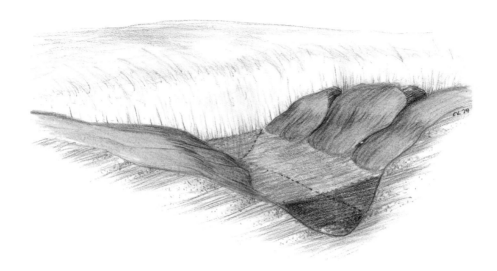

This illustration depicts a receding glacier that carved out a U-shaped valley that is beginning to fill with water. *Illustration by Christopher Loomis (loomisart.wordpress.com).*

This image shows the terminal moraine along the southern tip of Keuka Lake, which is the farthest point of advancement made by the glacier that formed this lake. *Photo by Bill Hecht.*

The early buds on this grapevine are susceptible to the erratic temperatures often associated with spring in the Finger Lakes. The moderating effect of the lakes keeps buds from breaking too early and risking damage from unexpected dips in temperature. *Courtesy of Heron Hill Winery.*

plow their way down the rivers, bulldozing its shallow V-shaped river valleys into deep U-shaped valleys of ice and debris. Once the ice age ended and the glaciers melted, we were left with a region of deep, narrow lakes where the rivers once flowed, surrounded by fertile glacial till.

The effect of this landscape is what has impacted the cultivators of the region. The lakes, because of their significant depth, serve as temperature moderators. The two deepest, Seneca and Cayuga, are approximately 650 and 425 feet deep, respectively, and almost never freeze over completely. This provides a blanket of warm condensation over their shores during the end of harvest and throughout the winter. In autumn, it protects crops from an early frost and can help lengthen the growing season to up to two to four weeks. During the winter, the lakes further protect the dormant plants from any severe temperature dips that might come through the region. Lastly, in the spring, the lakes moderate the vastly inconsistent modulations of temperatures in March, April and May and protect delicate buds from popping too early.

This implicit protection plan offered by Mother Nature has provided a special environment for the people of this region to nurture the land, and be rewarded with an annual abundance of fresh bounty of unusual variety, for what is considered to be a cool-growing region.

That is what this book celebrates. Each chapter will explore the impact that this region had on the people who have lived here and experienced its bounty over the millennia. It will share recipes, created by some of the most talented chefs in the region, that represent each time period. Each recipe is paired with currently available wines that go beautifully with the recipes and show off how good it gets in the Finger Lakes.

Chapter 1

THE FIRST PEOPLE OF THE FINGER LAKES

The Iroquois and the Three Sisters

The first known people to come to the Finger Lakes arrived from Asia across the Bering Strait land bridge over ten thousand years ago during the Paleolithic period and then migrated from the western part of the continent. Referred to as Paleo-Indians, these people were nomadic hunter-gathers who gathered berries and nuts and hunted big game such as mastodons, whose fossilized skeletons have been found in the region. The first Native Americans to settle in the Finger Lakes were the Lamoka Indians, who lived between Lamoka and Waneta Lakes dating back to 3,500 B.C. in what is considered the oldest prehistoric village in New York. They were hunter-gatherers as well, as evidenced by the Lamoka archaeological site, which contained food scraps of deer, acorns, turkey, pigeon and fish.[1] It wasn't until the Iroquois[2] arrived that the fertile land

---

1. The Lamoka archaeological site is a National Historic Landmark and has been recognized by the National Park Service as being the "first clear evidence of an archaic hunting and gathering culture in the Northeastern United States."

2. The Iroquois referred to themselves as Haudenosuaunee. This translates to "the people of the long house," describing the houses they built consisting of wood poles, thatched roofs and bark-woven walls. These houses were, on average, eighty feet long and housed up to sixty people.

of the Finger Lakes was predominantly used for farming. The tribes that eventually made up the Iroquois Confederacy are believed to have migrated to what is now New York State approximately one thousand years ago. The confederacy grew to be one of the most powerful political and economic entities in the Northeast from the time European colonists arrived to America through the Revolutionary War. The five tribes of the original Iroquois Confederacy formed in the mid-1400s were the Mohawk, Onondaga, Oneida, Seneca and Cayuga. The Tuscarora tribe joined the confederacy in 1720. The Seneca and Cayuga tribes were the Iroquois of the Finger Lakes, living in villages around the lakes that now bear their name. In fact, the name "Finger Lakes" is derived from a Native American legend that holds that the Great Spirit blessed the region by laying his hand on the land. The imprints from his fingers filled with water and became the Finger Lakes.

The Iroquois were agricultural people with agricultural villages. Farmed crops represented 50 percent of their food and, because of their agricultural success, provided the foundation of their power. The Iroquois were a matriarchal society, in which women held important government and sociocultural roles. Women held the knowledge, controlled all aspects of farming in the villages and were the source of the skills and expertise. They were highly sophisticated and productive farmers. Corn, supplemented by beans and squash, was the foundation of the Iroquois physical and spiritual life. Known as the "Three Sisters," these three crops were grown together in what is known today as a polyculture, a system in which each sister (or plant) serves a role in the mutual benefit of all three. The Iroquois visualized the Three Sisters as their sustainers who were put on earth by the Sky Woman to ensure their survival.

Below is an interpretation of an online presentation given by Dr. Jane Mt. Pleasant, a Cornell University professor of agriculture and descendant of the Toscarara, in which she describes the spiritual relationship of the Three Sisters and their functional purpose as a food source to the Iroquois:

The first sister is Corn. Corn is the elder sister. She stands up tall and straight. She wears a hat at the top, and her face is the ear. She is serious, important and responsible. She is the engine of the trio. As a food source, she produces the largest amount of calories and energy, as well some protein. She is a very productive and competitive crop, providing weed and insect

Historic marker located near the DEC boat launch site between Lamoka and Waneta Lakes. *Photo by Laura Winter Falk.*

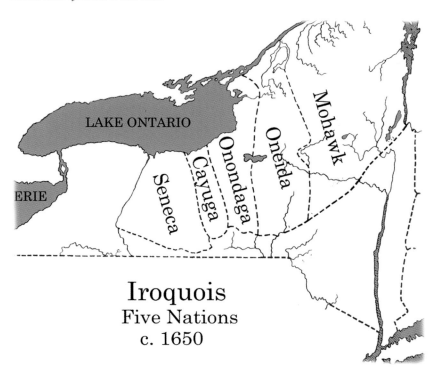

This map illustrates the geographic boundaries of the Five Nations of the Iroquois Confederacy circa 1650. The Tuscarora nation is not depicted in this map, as it did not join the confederacy until 1720. *Public domain.*

This is an example of a Three Sisters mound, depicting how corn, beans and squash were planted together in the mutually beneficial polyculture system used by the Iroquois. *Courtesy of Melissa Balding of Photo Bones.*

resistance, and support to the other plants. The second sister is Bean. Bean is shy and twines herself around the legs of her elder sister, occasionally peaking out from behind. Bean provides large amounts of protein to the Iroquois diet, as well as essential amino acids corn does not contain.[3] She also provides nitrogen to the other sisters, by converting nitrogen from the air into a form in the soil that the plants need to survive. The third sister is Squash. She is the little one. She stays close to the ground, is kind of impish and wild, spreads herself all over the place and is always getting into trouble. In addition to being a significant source of calories, Squash also provides valuable vitamins, minerals, oils and protein to the diet. Her low, wide leaves suppress weeds from growing around their space, capture sunlight and preserve moisture in the soil.

The Iroquois' polyculture system resulted in their being a very extensive agriculture power. Reports from European diaries and journals from the 1700s have described Iroquois villages as being surrounded by large fields of corn with storage buildings containing up to 1 million bushels of corn grain. They were better farmers than the colonists and enjoyed a high standard of living due to their level of production.[4]

In addition to growing their food, Iroquois were also hunters and gatherers. Men hunted bears, elk, deer, rabbits and wolves with bows and arrows. They trapped wild turkeys and ducks and caught fish with huge nets. Women and children gathered nuts, fruits, wild vegetables and mushrooms. Sunflower seeds were gathered and pressed to make oil for frying. They also tapped maple trees in the early spring to make syrup. Maple syrup was a special treat to the Iroquois. Below is the legend of how it was discovered, as told in a 1950s publication titled *The Maple Sugar Book*:

Woksis (an Iroquois Chief) was going hunting one day early in March. He yanked his tomahawk from the tree where he had hurled it the night before, and went off for the day. The weather turned warm and the gash in the tree, a maple, dripped sap into a vessel that happened to stand close to the trunk.

---

3. This is known nutritionally as "protein complementation" and is a very important dietary necessity for vegetarians.

4. Today, the Iroquois White Corn Project, run by the Friends of Ganondagan, aims "to restore the farming, consumption, and distribution of a traditional, nutritious, low-glycemic index Iroquois white corn…providing a supply of white corn to Native communities and the community at large, while creating a sustainable market for Haudenosaunee farmers." Visit the Ganondagon historical site, in the town of Victor, and experience where thousands of Seneca lived three hundred years ago. For more information, go to www.ganondagan.org.

An artistic rendering of the Three Sisters: corn, beans and squash.
Illustration by Christopher Loomis (loomisart.wordpress.com).

Woksis's wife, toward evening, needed water in which to boil their dinner. She saw the trough full of sap and thought that would save her a trip to get water. Anyway, she was a careful woman and didn't like to waste anything. She tasted it and found it good—a little sweet, but not bad. So she used it for cooking water. Woksis, when he came home from hunting, scented the inimitable maple aroma, and from far off knew that something especially good was stewing. The water had boiled down to syrup, which sweetened their meal with maple. So, says the legend, was the happy practice inaugurated.

Many of the food practices and recipes, like maple syrup making, were shared with the early Europeans who passed through the region and later became a part of American tradition and industry.

RECIPE AND WINE PAIRING

Honoring the Iroquois and the Three Sisters is Mary Jane Challen-Kircher and her interpretation of Finger Lakes Three Sisters Soup. Mary Jane owns and operates the Copper Oven, a wood-fired pizza oven and bistro located at her parent's winery, Cayuga Ridge Estate Winery on the west side of Cayuga Lake. Since coming onto the scene in 2010, Mary Jane has redefined Finger Lakes pizza. Unique combinations of all locally sourced ingredients on top of hand-stretched dough fired at 850 degrees in a six-thousand-pound French clay oven create a pizza so amazing that people travel from all over just to experience her individual masterpieces with creative names such as "Figgy Piggy" and "Fun-Guy" (mushroom pizza).

Mary Jane describes how she came up with the recipe:

Cooking in the Finger Lakes is always an adventure. With so many local farms focusing on sustainable growth and heirloom plant varieties, there are many lessons to be learned when translating these bounties to the plate. This holds especially true when exploring food culture of the Iroquois people. As a minor in Native American studies during college, I have always been interested in Haudenosaunee culture. Working on this project was the first opportunity I had to delve back into that interest in a number of years. A quick search led me to the Iroquois White Corn Project. Operated by the Friends of Ganondagan and based in Victor, New York, their beautifully packaged white-hulled corn is "developed from plants with roots reaching back more than 2,000 years." This is truly amazing! Soaking the corn overnight and cooking the kernels on low heat for about 5 hours allows them to split open, revealing a tender vegetable that manages to hold its firmness and is still packed with nutrition and flavor. Utilizing organic black beans from Cayuga Pure Organics, for their earthy flavor and contrasting color, and a blend of

Mary Jane Challen-Kircher in front of her Copper Oven, where she creates locally sourced wood-fired pizzas at Cayuga Ridge Estate Winery throughout the growing season. *Photo by Laura Winter Falk.*

Mary Jane Challen-Kircher's Three Sisters Soup paired with Cayuga Ridge Estate Winery Chardonnay in front of the burning hearth of the Copper Oven. *Photo by Robyn Wishna.*

butternut, buttercup and hubbard squash puree from my 2013 garden via my freezer, allowed for a stock rich in color and naturally sweet in taste. In creating a soup, I aspired to make a dish that allows the Three Sisters of corn, beans and squash to complement each other and exist in the same space, none overtaking or outshining the other—each component with it's own role to play in texture and flavor, with the culmination of all three portions leading to a sum greater than its individual parts.

Mary Jane and her parents, Tom and Susie Challen, worked together to select the wine to pair with her recipe. The Three Sisters Soup is paired with the Cayuga Ridge Barrel Select Chardonnay. The wine on its own has a wonderful earthen vanilla flavor that is a fabulous choice for this rustic dish. When consumed with the soup, the wine's natural creaminess integrates seamlessly with all the components in the recipe. Like most traditional Chardonnays, the wine has undergone a process called malolactic fermentation, in which malic acid is converted to lactic acid. Lactic acid is the natural acid in dairy products, and this conversion creates a creamy texture in the wine. The rustic corn flavor is accentuated in the wine's finish, as is the smoky flavor in the bacon garnish.

THREE SISTERS SOUP
(paired with Cayuga Ridge Chardonnay)

Serves 10–12

INGREDIENTS

2 cups dried Iroquois white-hulled corn
2 cups dried Cayuga Pure Organics black beans
6–8 cups homemade chicken stock
2 tablespoons beef demi-glace
1 large Vidalia onion
2 tablespoons butter
2 cups cooked squash puree
¼ cup heavy cream
thick-cut bacon, chopped, to garnish
chives, chopped, to garnish

INSTRUCTIONS

1. Soak corn 8 hours. Soak beans 4 hours.
2. Cook corn on low heat in water for 6 hours, or in slow cooker on low overnight.
3. Cook beans on medium low heat for 1 hour.
4. Sauté chopped Vidalia onion in 2 tablespoons butter.
5. Add half the chicken stock, the beef demi-glace and the cream. Add squash puree. Blend all components in a blender.
6. Add cooked corn and cooked beans to soup mixture. Add ladles of remaining stock as necessary in order to achieve a thick, stew-like consistency.
7. Ladle into deep bowls. Garnish with bacon and chives.

Chapter 2

THE LATE 1700s

The War, Postwar Homesteads and When the Apple Was King

The onset of the Revolutionary War brought the Finger Lakes to the attention of the competing sides. Originally, the Iroquois Confederacy tried to stay neutral, but pressure eventually forced the tribes to make individual decisions. The Oneida and Tuscarara sided with the colonists. The Mohawk, Onondaga, Seneca and Cayuga chose to remain loyal to the British and became a direct threat to the colonists. In a forceful move to destroy the impact of the British-Indian alliance, General George Washington decided in 1779 to order Generals John Sullivan and James Clinton into the Finger Lakes, with their sole mission being the removal of Iroquois out of the region to limit their support and provision supply to the British. Below are passages taken directly from General Washington's orders:

> *The expedition you are appointed to command is to be directed against the hostile tribes of the six nations of Indians, with their associates and adherents. The immediate objects are the total destruction and devastation of their settlements and the capture of as many prisoners of every age and sex as possible.*

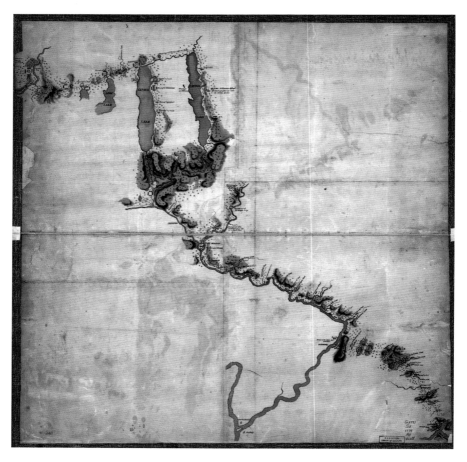

Map depicting the expedition route of General John Sullivan's army against the Cayuga and Seneca nations in the Finger Lakes region, June 18–September 16, 1779. *Library of Congress image provided by Robert Spiegelman of www.sullivanclinton.com.*

I would recommend that some post in the center of the Indian Country should be occupied with all expedition, with a sufficient quantity of provision; whence parties should be detached to lay waste all the settlements around, with instructions to do it in the most effectual manner; that the country may not be merely overrun but destroyed.

According to Sullivan's official report, the number of towns the army destroyed amounted to forty, and the quantity of corn destroyed amounted to "160,000 bushels, with a vast quantity of vegetables of every kind." As

JOURNALS

OF THE

MILITARY EXPEDITION

of

MAJOR GENERAL JOHN SULLIVAN

AGAINST THE

Six Nations of Indians

IN 1779

WITH RECORDS OF

Centennial Celebrations

PREPARED PURSUANT TO CHAPTER 361, LAWS
OF THE STATE OF NEW YORK, OF 1885,

BY

FREDERICK COOK,

SECRETARY OF STATE

AUBURN, N.Y.
· KNAPP, PECK & THOMSON · PRINTERS ·
·1887·

Cover of General John Sullivan's collection of journals that include the details of his military expedition against the Cayuga and Seneca nations in the Finger Lakes. *Public domain*.

Small towns began to form during the late 1700s based on their ability to mill the crop of the Finger Lakes homesteaders. Gristmills were built along creeks and waterfalls. New towns, such as Ithaca, Watkins Glen, Honeoye Falls and Moravia, developed around them. Mill owners would trade use of the mill for a portion of the flour produced. Pictured above and opposite is the Old Mill, which served as the gristmill for the hamlet of Enfield Falls from 1839 to 1916. The above picture was taken in 1915 during its final years of operation. (Image courtesy of Friends of Robert H. Treman State Park.) The picture on the opposite page was taken in 2012 after it had been restored. (Photo by Tony Ingraham.) The Old Mill is listed on the National Register of Historic Places, and you can see the Old Mill and its workings when visiting Robert H. Treman State Park in Ithaca.

a result, the surviving Iroquois were moved to reservations near Buffalo, Ontario and as far as Oklahoma.[5]

After the Revolutionary War, both Massachusetts and New York competed for the claim of the fertile Finger Lakes land. The resulting Treaty of Hartford awarded sovereignty and jurisdiction to New York but gave Massachusetts preemptive right to negotiate with the Iroquois for clear title of the land. Speculators purchased land rights from Massachusetts and began negotiating land titles in the western Finger Lakes with the Iroquois for resale to settlers. In addition, the land comprising the eastern Finger Lakes became part of the Military Tract of Central New York, which set aside 2 million acres of land to compensate New York soldiers after the

5. Today, there is a band of the Cayuga tribe living on reclaimed land in Seneca Falls and Aurora. There are five Seneca reservations in New York State, but none of them are in the Finger Lakes.

Revolutionary War. Tracts were divided and parceled, establishing many homesteads of sustenance farmers and their families. Homesteaders grew wheat, corn, vegetables and fruit. Many cooking techniques of the settler women were borrowed from the Iroquois. They learned to cook Indian corn, pumpkins, squash, beans and succotash. They also learned about picking cranberries, huckleberries, wild plums, roots and herbs. Drying of all fruits and vegetables was very important, as glass for canning was expensive. These dried items were indispensable in the winter, as they provided the settlers with important nutrients to keep them healthy when times were lean.

Of all the fruit grown during this time, none was more important to the farmers than the apple. In the 1600s, when colonists arrived from Europe, the only apple they found in America was the crab apple. Since the apple was a particular favorite of the English (the word "apple" derives from the Old English word *aeppel*), they imported apple seeds to plant in their new home. They also traded the seeds with the Iroquois, so apple trees were well established in the Finger Lakes by the late 1600s. By the time the European American settlers moved into the region, the apple trees planted by the Iroquois were in abundance and producing dependable fruit that appeared

Above: Apple orchards with gorgeous fruit abound all over the Finger Lakes in autumn. There are over forty u-pick orchards throughout the region where you can choose from a vast number of New York varieties. For a full listing of u-pick farms in the Finger Lakes, visit www.ediblefingerlakes.com/u-pick-farms. *Courtesy of www. visitfingerlakes.com.*

Left: Cider mills like this one were an indispensable piece of equipment on the farms of Finger Lakes homesteaders. *Public domain.*

in the Finger Lakes family diet in many forms throughout the year. The autumn harvest brought fresh apples and juice. As the year progressed, the fruit's long shelf life allowed fresh apples well into the winter, and its preserved versions of apple butter, sauce and dried apples appeared in many recipes. In addition to its food variations, one of the apple's most important forms was as a beverage. Early settlers preferred not to drink water, as it often made them sick and led to dysentery. On the other hand, apple cider in all its forms did not make them sick (except if consumed in overabundance, of course), could be drunk all throughout the year in its fermented form and facilitated much-needed relaxation after a day of backbreaking work in the fields. Even children would drink ciderkin (a diluted version of hard cider) to keep them hydrated and healthy. Sweet cider, hard cider, apple vinegar and applejack[6] were all bartered and traded for other goods, as well as used as a unit of exchange to pay doctors, teachers and ministers. This resulted in an estimated per capita consumption of hard apple cider of around thirty-plus gallons per person per year. By the late 1700s, almost all Finger Lakes homesteads had a cider press.

Another important homestead crop in the Finger Lakes was buckwheat. Buckwheat was a very common crop to Finger Lakes settlers in the late 1700s because it was very versatile and easy to grow. Because of its ability to tolerate poor soils, it was often used in fields where no other crop could successfully be cultivated. It then subsequently improved them by adding important nutrients back into ground. It also served as a very good cover and second-season crop due to its short growing season. Birkett Mills, in the village of Penn Yan on Keuka Lake, began milling buckwheat in 1797. Today, Penn Yan is considered the buckwheat capital of America, and Birkett Mills, in continuous operation for over two hundred years, is the world's largest manufacturer of buckwheat products.

Birkett Mills and the Penn Yan Buckwheat Festival holds the *Guinness Book of World Records* title for the world's largest pancake. The pancake, twenty-eight feet and one inch in diameter, was cooked at the festival on September 21, 1987. Jennifer Wright, who was at the record-breaking event, posted her experience on roadsideamerica.com. She wrote:

> *I ate this thing! The batter was mixed in a (clean) cement mixer, poured into the griddle (I think it had a metal lip) and heated over a large fire pit.*

---

6. Applejack was a distilled version of apple cider that was created when hard cider was left outside in the winter. The water in hard cider would freeze and then be removed, thus concentrating the alcohol levels.

The world's largest pancake griddle used to cook the world's largest pancake stands twenty-seven feet in diameter and is on display at Birkett Mills in Penn Yan. *Courtesy of Birkett Mills.*

When it was time for flipping, a matching-sized griddle was placed and secured on top, and the thing was flipped with a crane. The "pancake" was more like a 4-inch tall square of cake, served with syrup.

People can go to the Birkett Mills in Penn Yan and see the record-breaking griddle, which is on display on the side of the building.

RECIPE AND WINE PAIRING

Celebrating the ubiquitous and important nature of the apple and buckwheat of late 1700s Finger Lakes is a recipe of apple dumplings. Apple dumplings, a staple of eighteenth-century cooking, takes on a savory twist in Samantha Buyskes's interpretation. Samantha has been a champion of the Finger Lakes local food scene since 2002, when she opened her restaurant, Simply Red, in Trumansburg. Samantha serves as a culinary ambassador to the region. She has appeared as a contestant on the Food Network series *Chopped*, organizes pop-up kitchen appearances throughout the region, hosts monthly cooking classes as part of Experience! The Finger Lakes' Farm-to-Table Wine and Cooking Adventure and participates in a number of community outreach programs aimed at food education, skill development and combating local hunger. Samantha's signature style, which combines her South African upbringing with her passion for our region, integrates the Finger Lakes' seasonal harvest with her unique spice blends.

Here is what Samantha had to say about her interpretation of the traditional apple dumpling:

The apple dumpling evokes memories for most of those growing up as a child here in the Finger Lakes. At the peak of the fall season, one is left to daydream of everything apple. In this recipe, I had fun adding buckwheat, an indigenous grain in this region, to complement the bacon, cheddar and golden raisins. I love to consider ways to bring this unique flavor to life.

I paired Samantha's savory apple dumpling with Village White from Bet the Farm Winery, located on the east shore of Cayuga Lake. Owner Nancy Tisch and her husband, Kit Kalfs, operate Bet the Farm not only as a winery but also

Chef Samantha Buyskes surrounded by the spices that define her signature style of cooking. *Photo by Dylan Buyskes.*

Samantha Buyskes's Old-Fashioned Savory Apple Dumpling paired with Bet the Farm Village White. *Photo by Robyn Wishna.*

as a gourmet shop specializing in upstate New York products. In addition to the name "Village White" being perfectly suited to represent the small villages of the Finger Lakes during this era, the wine itself is a wonderful complement to this recipe. Village White is a blend of two French-American hybrid grapes: Cayuga White and Vidal. On its own, the wine gives off wonderful crisp apple aromas and flavors. When it is paired with the dumpling, the honey and apple notes in the wine are enhanced. The flavors of Sam's unique spice blend and the smoky saltiness of the bacon continue through the finish of the wine, egging you on to the next bite. The buckwheat, which adds its unique earthiness to the dumpling, is showcased when paired with this wine.

OLD-FASHIONED SAVORY APPLE DUMPLINGS
(paired with Bet the Farm Village White)

Yields 4 dumplings

INGREDIENTS

SAUCE
1 cup water
⅔ cup sugar
¼ teaspoon cinnamon
2 tablespoons butter

DUMPLINGS
2½ cups flour
½ cup buckwheat
1½ teaspoons salt
1 cup shortening
12–16 tablespoons milk
4 medium-size apples

Combine the three ingredients below together for filling:

12 ounces of grated cheddar
4–6 pieces of bacon, cooked and diced
1 cup raisins

SUGAR AND SPICE MIX
½ cup of sugar
1 teaspoon each of ground cinnamon, mace, ginger and clove

Process

1. Preheat oven to 425 degrees.
2. In a small saucepot, combine the water, sugar, cinnamon and butter. Bring to a boil and stir until the butter melts completely. Remove from heat and let cool while you make the dumplings.
3. In a large bowl, combine the flour, buckwheat, salt and shortening. Mix with your fingers until dough has a grainy texture (will look sort of like cornmeal). Add the milk and mix until combined.
4. Roll out dough to ⅛-inch thickness on a well-floured surface. Cut into 4 large squares.
5. Peel and core your apples with a nice, big hole for the filling and then stuff with the cheddar, bacon and raisin mixture.
6. Place one apple on each square of dough. Sprinkle cinnamon and sugar over top of the apple and then gently wrap dough around apple, sealing edges with a little water. Don't worry if the dough doesn't completely enclose around the apples—just do the best you can.
7. Place the dumplings in a greased pan and then pour the sauce over the dumplings and around the sides of the pan. Sprinkle with sugar and spice mix as well.
8. Bake for 40 minutes until golden brown.

There are diverse applications for this recipe:

For breakfast, serve it with a sunny-side-up egg
For lunch, serve with a nice tossed green salad and a light, bright vinaigrette.
For dinner, serve it with some grilled asparagus and a nice thick-cut pan-seared pork chop.

Slow-Ass Spiced and Spiked Apple Gingerbread
(paired with Sheldrake Point Late Harvest Riesling)

Samantha's spiced apple gingerbread is paired with Sheldrake Point Winery's Late Harvest Riesling. Sheldrake Point, located on the west side of Cayuga Lake, has received significant international recognition for its

Chef Samantha's Slow-Ass Spiced and Spiked Apple Gingerbread paired with Sheldrake Point Late Harvest Riesling. *Photo by Robyn Wishna.*

dessert Rieslings, both in the Late Harvest style and with its traditional ice wine. On its own, this wine has an infectious, mouthwatering acidity that is balanced with honey and apricot flavors. When the Riesling is paired with the gingerbread, there is an initial explosion of apple, clove and ginger flavor. The vibrant acidity of the wine then cuts into the sweetness of the dessert and pulls out the flavor of the caramel. The ending is a finish of spicy cloves and nutmeg left in your mouth to linger.

For a more historically oriented pairing, you can substitute the Late Harvest Riesling for Sheldrake Point's Ice Apple wine. For this wine, repeated freezing and thawing cycles are used to remove layers of ice and concentrate the sugars in the juice before fermenting. You can also choose one of the local Finger Lakes hard apple ciders, like Bellwether Hard Cider's Black Magic, which is a semisweet hard apple cider with black currant juice added.

Here is what Samantha has to say about the origins of this dessert:

As for the gingerbread, this is one of my favorite recipes that have been around since I opened the Trumansburg restaurant. Inspired by a jar of "Slow Ass" brand blackstrap molasses I found in a Florida grocery store, I couldn't resist keeping the name (and the ingredient) as I developed my recipe. I always told my guests not to be shy and ask for it by its full name. An array of autumn spices awakens the taste buds in this rustic apple cake. Its best baked during local apple harvest. I like to jack up the spices with the rich flavors of dark rum. Serve warm and piled with fresh whipped cream.

Serves 6

For the cake batter:

1 cup cornmeal	½ cup raisins
1 cup flour	2 apples cut into chunks, skin on
1½ tablespoon ground cinnamon	¼ cup granulated sugar
1½ tablespoon ground allspice	½ cup vegetable oil
1½ tablespoon ground ginger	1 egg
1 tablespoon ground clove	¼ cup blackstrap molasses
½ tablespoon salt	¼ cup dark rum
½ tablespoon baking powder	¼ cup maple syrup
½ tablespoon baking soda	

For the caramel sauce:
½ pound white granulated sugar
3 cups heavy cream
1 cinnamon stick
¼ cup fresh apple cider

PROCESS

For the cake batter:
1. Mix all the dry ingredients together and then add the raisins and apples.
2. Whisk together all the wet ingredients and then combine with the dry ingredients.
3. Scrape the batter into a 9-inch baking pan (sprayed with nonstick cooking spray) and bake in a pre-heated oven for 45 minutes at 375 degrees.

For the caramel sauce:
1. Place the sugar in a heavy-bottom pot on medium heat and continuously stir with a wooden spoon (the sugar will begin to slowly melt and caramelize).
2. Pour in two cups of heavy cream very slowly. (It will sputter and boil up, and it might even clump, but have no fear. Simply turn the heat down to low and stir occasionally as the cream comes to temperature). Add in the cinnamon stick and apple cider and simmer for about 15 minutes.
3. Allow to cool and then pour into a sealed container (the caramel sauce and apple cider will separate slightly while being stored—just stir it up every time you use it).

To serve:
1. Slice the cake into 6 servings.
2. Place into bowls and top each serving with ⅓ cup caramel sauce.
3. Whip remaining cup of heavy cream into soft peaks and top each dessert.
4. Sprinkle a mix of cinnamon and brown sugar to finish.

Chapter 3

THE 1800s

THE INDUSTRIALIZATION OF A REGION AND THE BIRTH OF THE GRAPE AND WINE INDUSTRY

The homesteading era, and the relative isolation of the new white settlers of the Finger Lakes, came to an abrupt end in the early 1800s with the building of the Erie Canal. The primary New York waterways of New York City to Lake Champlain via the Hudson River, and the Oswego River and Mohawk Rivers to Lake Ontario, were always important trade routes for the Iroquois, fur traders, missionaries and colonizers during the early development of the colonies. With our young country expanding westward, it became ever more important to develop efficient routes of commerce to support the growing populations. Thus, in 1817, Governor Dewitt Clinton and the New York State legislature approved the construction of the Erie Canal. The canal was fully funded by New York State with no federal support, as President Thomas Jefferson rejected investing in the project, calling it "a little short of madness."

The canal was certainly ambitious and very expensive, cutting through mountains and limestone and requiring fifty locks along the 360-mile route to account for a six-hundred-foot rise in land elevation from Albany to Buffalo. In fact, during its planning and construction, the project was ridiculed as

The Erie Canal Aqueduct over the Genesee River in Rochester, circa 1888. *Public domain.*

"Clinton's Folly" and "Clinton's Ditch." It turned out, however, to be quite the opposite. According to the Erie Canalway National Heritage Corridor: "The Erie Canal was North America's most successful and influential public works project. The Erie Canal built the Empire State…and secured New York City's position as the nation's busiest port, most populous city, and foremost seat of commerce and finance." It also directly affected the growth and economic development of the communities along its path, creating thriving towns and cities. Such was the case in the Finger Lakes, with the Cayuga-Seneca Canal and the smaller Crooked Lake Canal linking the region to the main Erie artery. Cities that had direct access to these canals— such as Ithaca and Watkins Glen to the south and Canandaigua, Geneva and Seneca Falls to the north—flourished. The fertile land of the region provided the landscape for new agricultural industries that shared the Finger Lakes bounty with people from New York City to Chicago. Geneva was known throughout the nation for its nurseries. Rochester was known as the "Flour City" due to its numerous flour mills powered by waterfalls on the Genesee River. Because of its temperate climate and proximity to the ports on Crooked Lake Canal, Yates County, which encompasses western Seneca Lake, northern Keuka Lake and eastern Canandaigua Lake, became known as the "Fruit Basket of New York State." Commercial orchards of peaches, plums, apricots and, of course, apples were all transported first by canal and then later, when the railroads were introduced, by rail car, thus moving the highly desirable fresh fruit quickly and efficiently into the hands of grateful consumers. Incidentally, by the 1800s, cider's place in American homes began to wane. Homestead cider production went from 96 percent of farms in 1790 to 48 percent in 1860. The industrialization boom of the region led to a significant increase in the number of jobs available in fast-growing towns and cities. This resulted in many people moving from homesteads into towns and thus abandoning their orchards. Furthermore, beer (a favorite beverage that was originally expensive to make and hard to import from Europe) became accessible with an increase in breweries and pubs in the local cities.

With the public palate in transition, the opportunity for the introduction of domestic wine was ripe, and the birth of the most successful of all commercial fruit ventures in the Finger Lakes began. The first to plant grapes in the Finger Lakes was Reverend William Bostwick of Hammondsport, who, in 1829, planted Catawba and Isabella grapes for his rectory. For many years, Reverend Bostwick was known to be the only grape grower in the region. He encouraged others to plant grapes in the region by sharing cuttings of his vines with his neighbors. J.W. Prentiss, known to be the first commercial grape grower and wine producer in the region, planted these vine cuttings of Isabella and Catawba in 1836 and sold them as table grapes first to regional cities and later to the eastern U.S. market due to demand and ease of distribution. By 1860, three thousand acres of grapevines grew along the shores of Canandaigua, Keuka and Seneca Lakes. Barges, each carrying sixty-five tons of grapes, made their way through the Crooked Lake Canal and the Seneca-Cayuga Canal en route to the Erie Canal.

Reverend Bostwick also was known to encourage his neighbors to experiment in making wine from their grapes. This was quite frowned upon by the growing temperance movement in the region, which accused the reverend of "inventing tools of the devil."[7] However, despite the temperance resistance, the call for Finger Lakes wine could not be ignored, and the first

---

7. According to Richard Sherer, in an article written about the early grape pioneers of the Finger Lakes, people were so infuriated with the reverend and his promotion of early winemaking that when he moved to Illinois in 1843, someone ripped all of his rectory grapevines out of the ground.

Hand-harvesting grapes in the vineyards along Keuka Lake. *Courtesy of Hammondsport Public Library*.

Illustration of Pleasant Valley Wine Company (U.S. Bonded Winery #1) and its vineyards. *Courtesy of Hammondsport Public Library*.

known shipment of Finger Lakes wine to New York City was made by J.W. Prentiss under the label of Highland Cottage Wine. Unfortunately, Mr. Prentiss's skills as a winemaker were not as great as his skills as a businessman, and by 1860, his wines were not heard of again. But appetites were whet by the unique and fruitful flavors of the Finger Lakes wine, so when the right winemaking skills were brought to Keuka Lake in the 1860s, the Finger Lakes winemaking industry exploded.

The first winery in the United States to be recognized as a commercial winery was the Hammondsport and Pleasant Valley Wine Company, incorporated as U.S. Bonded Winery #1 in 1860.[8] The principle landowner, Charles Davenport Champlin, recognizing the cooler climate of the region and its advantages for making sparkling wine, made the calculated decision to focus on producing champagne made from the Native American grapes that had been thriving in the region, namely Isabella and Catawba. Davenport hired brothers Jules and Joseph Masson, winemakers from the Champagne region of France, to oversee all wine production. Their product, Great Western Champagne, was thusly named when well-known wine connoisseur Marshall Wilder declared it to be "the Great Champagne of the Western World."[9] By 1867, Pleasant Valley began introducing its champagne to Europe via international wine competitions. In 1873, it was awarded first prize in a competition in Vienna, Austria. The demand for Finger Lakes champagne skyrocketed, and a quick succession of wineries opened around Keuka and Seneca Lakes. Wineries like Urbana Wine Co., Widmer and Taylor expanded their wine production, developing still wines to be used as sacramental wines, as well as popular fortified wines like ports and sherries.[10] By the end of the nineteenth century, there were more than twenty thousand acres of vineyards around the Finger Lakes and more than fifty wineries producing over 7 million bottles of champagne. The Finger Lakes became

8. All commercial wineries in the United States are required to purchase a bond equal to the maximum quantity of wine that can be produced in their winery.

9. Back in the 1860s, the French government had yet to seek to protect the use of the term "champagne" outside of the Champagne region in France, so any winery could call its sparkling wine "champagne." Today, no wine producer in the United States can use the term "champagne" on its label unless the product and label were approved prior to 2006. Therefore, due to its place in history, Great Western Champagne is one of the few U.S.-produced sparkling wines still allowed to use the "champagne" label.

10. Fortified wine is made by fermenting grape juice and then stopping the fermentation process by adding spirits such as brandy. The result is a wine that is around 18–20 percent alcohol.

Men bottling champagne at Hammondsport Wine Company. *Courtesy of Hammondsport Public Library.*

Workers around the wine press at White Top Winery. *Courtesy of Hammondsport Public Library.*

synonymous with American sparkling wine and produced twice as much sparkling wine than all the other states in the country combined. However, the growth of wine production in the Finger Lakes was running parallel with the growth of the temperance movement, which was about to bring the entire industry to a screeching halt.

In addition to the new wine industry, New York State agriculture was considered at its best in the mid-nineteenth century, according to Ulysses Hendrick in his 1933 book *A History of Agriculture in the State of New York*. Finger Lakes farmers were highly independent with money coming in from the sale of their farm products throughout the country. A wonderful description of a typical Finger Lakes farm in the late nineteenth century is depicted in the following passage from the Ontario County Agriculture Enhancement Board's website (www.fingerlakesagriculture.com):

A typical 1890s farm was about 50 acres in size and was highly diversified compared to the farms of today. They had about 13 cows, a few pigs and chickens plus a substantial garden. These commodities were used to feed the family and also to barter for other goods and services. This farm would also have a major enterprise that provided cash income to the operator. Hops, barley, milk, sheep, black raspberries, apples and grapes were the usual commodities. Milk was shipped to Canandaigua to one of the two breweries for processing. Sheep were raised for wool and meat; black raspberries were sold to manufacture a dye for use in Jello that was produced in Leroy, NY. Apples and black raspberries for "fresh" sales were dried and shipped to market, while grapes were sold as fresh and became the basis for the growing wine industry.

There was a high level of pride and respect for the farmers, who often held prominent positions in the community and in government. The formation of the New York State Agricultural Society in 1832 resulted in a number of initiatives that have significantly impacted Finger Lakes agriculture, one of the most significant being the formation of the College of Agriculture at Cornell University. Both Cornell University and the College of Agriculture were created via funds from the federal Morrill Land Grant Act. The act rewarded land or money from the sale of that land to each state in order to create a land-grant college with the purpose "to teach such branches of learning as are related to agriculture and the mechanic arts…in order to promote the liberal and practical education of the industrial classes in the several pursuits and professions in life."

COUNTRY FOOD AND DRINK

PROGRAMME

• • •

TOASTMASTER
Dr. Liberty Hyde Bailey

INVOCATION
Rev. Calvin H. French
Pastor, Madison Avenue Presbyterian Church

SPEAKERS
Hon. Arthur Mastick Hyde
*Secretary of the Department of Agriculture
of the United States*

Hon. Franklin Delano Roosevelt
Governor of the State of New York

Dancing — old and new
Reincarnations

MENU

Fruit Cup

Roast Turkey — Stuffing — Gravy
Mashed Potatoes — Squash in Shell

Plum Jelly — Pickles
Coleslaw

Johnnycake

Pumpkin Pie — Cheese
Coffee

YE OLDE-TIME FARM SUPPER GIVEN BY THE NEW YORK STATE
AGRICULTURAL SOCIETY IN HONOR OF THE ONE HUNDREDTH
ANNIVERSARY OF ITS FOUNDING, 1832–1932

219

Reproduction of the menu served at the 1932 Ye Olde-Tyme Farm Supper commemorating the 100th anniversary of the New York Agricultural Society. Dignitaries included Liberty Hyde Bailey, founder and first dean of the New York College of Agriculture; Arthur Mastick Hyde, secretary of the U.S. Department of Agriculture; and Franklin Delano Roosevelt, who was serving his final months as governor of New York State before being inaugurated as president of the United States in January 1933. *Image taken from* A History of Agriculture in the State of New York.

This achievement has inextricably linked the region to some of the best agricultural research and education in the country. In 1932, to commemorate its 100th anniversary, the Ag Society held a gala featuring an 1800s Olde-Tyme Farm Supper. In attendance were Arthur Hyde, then secretary of the U.S. Department of Agriculture, and Franklin Delano Roosevelt, then governor of New York.

Recipe and Wine Pairing

In honor of this important era in Finger Lakes history and the impact the New York State Agricultural Society has had on the region, I have asked Chef Brud Holland to re-create Ye Olde-Tyme Farm Supper served at the 1932 celebration of the 100th anniversary of the New York Agricultural Society. It is also fitting to pair the menu with sparkling wine. While technically there most likely was not sparkling wine served that night (as Prohibition was still in effect), there is no doubt that Finger Lakes Champagne, so gloriously celebrated in the 1800s, would have been flowing if it were legal. And so it will flow in our re-creation of the meal. I have selected three Finger Lakes sparkling wines that represent the glorious bubbly produced in our region: the original Great Western Champagne, still made from native labrusca grapes; Brut, made from the Cayuga White French-American hybrid grape created by Cornell University; and Pinot Noir Brut Rosé, made from Pinot Noir, one of the traditional French champagne grapes.

In the Finger Lakes, Brud Holland is affectionately known as the "mad scientist of the culinary world" for his love of cooking up new concepts in the kitchen. He is a serial food entrepreneur, having owned and operated a gourmet bakery and deli and been a vegetarian products manufacturer before serving as executive chef at Corning Incorporated, the Corning County Club and Red Newt Cellars Winery and Bistro. Brud now considers himself a "freelance chef" in the Finger Lakes, giving himself time to work on food-related projects for his company, Finger Lakes Made, that he wouldn't have time for if he was the full-time chef of a restaurant kitchen. With Finger Lakes Made, he farms herbs, produces balsamic vinegar and develops an array of custom condiments made from ingredients grown by small farms in the Finger Lakes. He is also a passionate culinary educator, teaching cooking classes around the region and at the 171 Cedar Arts Center in Corning.

Finger Lakes regional chef Brud Holland. *Photo by Stu Gallagher.*

Here is what Brud had to say about bringing this traditional menu to life in the current day:

> *In my cooking, I'm always tying things together. What I mean by this is I try to bring together the wine, the food and the culture that makes the Finger Lakes what it is today. Taking an old menu from the past is an easy way to highlight the connection that we have with those whose work laid the foundation for what is happening in the region today. Not surprising to me, the ingredients are virtually the same and are still grown on small family farms. In fact, many of the farmers I buy from have reintroduced old techniques, seed varieties and farming practices that their grandfathers and great-grandfathers used. Roasted turkey, pickles, jams and Johnnycakes are as delicious and easy to make today as they were almost two hundred years ago.*

Following is the Olde-Tyme Farm Supper menu from the 100th celebration of the New York State Agricultural Society.

First Course

FRUIT CUP
(paired with Hosmer Winery Brut Sparkling Wine)

Serves 6

We paired this Finger Lakes fruit cup with Brut Sparkling Wine from Hosmer Winery. Owners Cameron and Maren Hosmer have been growing grapes on the west side of Cayuga Lake since the late 1970s. Their beautiful sparkling wine is made from 100 percent Cayuga White grapes and produced in the classic *méthod champenoise*. This method involves two yeast fermentations, with the second taking place inside the bottle to trap the bubbles of carbon dioxide. Cayuga White made in this method makes a beautiful, creamy sparkling wine with wonderful aromas of apple and bread dough. Pairing this sparkler with fresh fruit is a celebration of the fruit in the wine and in the serving dish. The Cayuga White grape in the wine is accented by hints of apple and pear with a touch of the raspberry in the finish.

Main Course

ROAST TURKEY BREAST WITH HALF-BAKED MASHED POTATOES, SQUASH IN THE SHELL, JOHNNYCAKES, JAM AND PICKLES
(paired with Hosmer Winery Pinot Noir Brut Rosé)

Very few things go better with a traditional turkey dinner than Pinot Noir dry rosé. Make it a sparkling version, and now you really have a party! We once more turn to Hosmer Winery for this pairing, as its Pinot Noir Brut Rosé is perfect for this course. The delicate fruit flavors of the rosé accentuate the savory flavors of the turkey without dominating it. Add in the creamy potatoes and blackberry jam, and the wonderful berry fruit flavors in the wine start to shine. Once you have experienced how lively and flavorful this pairing is, you will never leave sparkling Pinot Noir off your Thanksgiving table again.

When creating this fruit cup, Chef Brud was careful to only use fruits that would have been available in the Finger Lakes in the 1830s. Fruit used: apples, grapes, pears and raspberries garnished with Finger Lakes garden-fresh chocolate mint. The fruit cup is paired with Hosmer Winery Brut Sparking Wine. *Photo by Robyn Wishna.*

Brud Holland's re-creation of the Ye Olde-Tyme Farm Supper main course of Roast Turkey with Mashed Potatoes, Squash in the Shell, Johnnycakes, Jam and Pickles paired with Hosmer Winery Pinot Noir Brut Rosé. *Photo by Robyn Wishna.*

ROASTED TURKEY BREAST WITH ROASTED CARROT SALT AND THYME GRAVY

Serves 6

INGREDIENTS

2½ to 3 pounds (boneless) turkey breast, skin on
Finger Lakes Made roasted carrot salt (or favorite dry rub mixture)
1½ cups chicken stock
1 tablespoon fresh thyme
1 tablespoon all-purpose flour
3 tablespoons Riesling

PROCESS

1. Sprinkle the turkey breast liberally with salt. Place on an oiled baking sheet with the skin side up. Score the skin in a crosshatch pattern with a sharp knife. Roast in a 375-degree oven for 1 hour or until the internal temperature reaches 155 degrees. Remove from the oven and place on a warm platter while making the gravy.
2. To make the gravy, add some of the chicken stock to the pan on which the turkey was roasted. Scrape the mixture into a small saucepan, add the thyme and remaining stock and reduce the liquid to about 1 cup by boiling on high heat.
3. In a small bowl, mix the flour and Riesling with a whisk. Add to the reduced stock and bring to a quick boil to thicken the gravy.
4. Slice turkey and serve with warm gravy.

HALF-BAKED MASHED POTATOES

Serves 4

INGREDIENTS

2 to 3 New York russet baker potatoes, peeled and cut into 1-inch cubes
¼ cup milk

¼ cup cream

2 tablespoons butter

10 turns of black pepper, freshly ground

2 to 3 New York russet baker potatoes, baked at 400 degrees until soft (about 45–50 minutes)

Process

1. In a 2-quart saucepan filled ¾ full with salted water, cook the potatoes until tender. Drain. To the same pan, add the milk, cream, butter and pepper and bring to a boil. Add the drained potatoes and mash, leaving a few lumps.
2. Scoop the baked potatoes and add to the mashed, carefully folding in to leave lumps.

Squash in the Shell

I love Brud's interpretation of the menu's Squash in the Shell. Instead of serving the squash in its natural shell (which I am sure is the way it was served both in the 1800s and at the 100th celebration dinner), he serves his squash in a pastry shell, adding his own modern-day twist.

Serves 6

FOR THE SHELL'S PASTRY DOUGH

1 cup Birkett Mills "Bessie" flour (pastry)

½ cup Farmer Ground all-purpose flour

½ cup butter, cut in tablespoon-sized pieces

1 teaspoon kosher salt

½ cup buttermilk

FOR THE FILLING

½ pound grated cheddar or Swiss cheese

½ cup zucchini

½ cup yellow squash

¼ cup red pepper, diced

1 tablespoon leaf parsley, roughly chopped

½ cup cream

½ cup whole milk

½ teaspoon kosher salt

2 eggs

Process:

1. In a large mixing bowl, combine the flours, butter and salt. Using your fingers or a pastry cutter, cut the butter into the flour until it resembles flakes the size and thickness of a dime. Add the buttermilk, reserving about 1 tablespoon to adjust the dough and stir with a fork until it forms a dough.* Refrigerate dough wrapped in plastic wrap for 15 minutes before rolling.

2. Divide dough into 6 pieces and roll on a floured surface into a 4-inch x 6-inch rectangle about ⅛ inch thick. Lay into greased 2½-inch x 4-inch square muffin pans.

3. In a large mixing bowl, mix the cheese, zucchini, squash, peppers and parsley. Fill each of the shells.

4. In another bowl, whisk together the cream, milk, salt and eggs. Pouring slowly, fill each shell to the top.

5. Place muffin pan into a 350-degree oven and bake for 30–35 minutes or until golden and the centers are firm and spongy. Cool for 15–20 minutes before serving. May be cut in half for smaller servings.

*PASTRY TIP: Different flour brands can have different levels of liquid absorption. If your pastry dough looks or feels dry, simply add 1 tablespoon of buttermilk to the dry areas and mix until the dough is soft and slightly tacky but not sticky.

Plum Jelly and Pickles

Brud makes all his own jams and pickles using 100 percent locally sourced ingredients. In this meal, he used his sweet cucumber and onion pickles and a wonderful wild blackberry jam.

Johnnycakes

Serves 6

Ingredients

½ cup Farmer Ground cornmeal
½ cup Birkett Mills "Bessie" flour
½ teaspoon kosher salt
½ cup buttermilk
1 tablespoon honey
1 egg
1 tablespoon fresh leaf parsley, roughly chopped
butter
bacon fat

Process

1. In a large bowl, whisk together the cornmeal, flour, salt, buttermilk, honey, egg and parsley until it makes a smooth batter.
2. In a cast-iron skillet on medium-high heat, add the butter and bacon fat. Using a portion scoop or tablespoon, make small, silver dollar–sized "pancakes" with the batter. Cook until golden brown on the first side (about 1½ minutes) and then turn and repeat for the second side. Serve hot from the pan with syrup or gravy. Keep warm in a 180-degree oven if making a larger recipe.

Dessert

Caramel Ginger Pumpkin Pie
(paired with Great Western Extra Dry Champagne)

Once again, I love Brud's interpretation of the original menu's offering of pumpkin pie with cheese. He puts the cheese in the pastry to make savory cheddar pastry chips that surround his ginger-pumpkin filling. Pairing this dessert with our third sparking wine, the traditional Great Western Extra Dry Champagne, marks the perfect finish to a great meal. The touch of sweetness in the wine complements the subtle sweet and savory components of the pie.

Serves 6

FOR THE CRUST

¾ cup Birkett Mills "Bessie" flour (pastry)
½ cup Farmer Ground all-purpose flour
1 teaspoon kosher salt
pinch sugar
1 stick butter, cut in tablespoon-sized pieces
¼ cup grated cheddar
⅓ cup whole milk

FOR THE FILLING

¼ cup sugar
2 tablespoons water
½ cup cream
1 pound roasted pumpkin
additional ¼ cup sugar
2 eggs
2 tablespoons ground dry ginger
milk

PROCESS

1. In a large bowl, add the flours, salt, sugar and butter. Using a pastry cutter or your fingers, cut the butter into the flour until it reaches the size and thickness of a dime.
2. Add the cheese and milk and mix into a soft, tacky dough. Dust with flour and roll onto a floured surface, rolling the dough to ¹⁄₁₆ inch thick. Cut into 1½- to 2-inch pieces. Place on a baking sheet and bake in a 375-degree oven until golden brown, about 15 minutes.
3. In a small saucepan on high heat, cook the sugar and water until the mixture turns dark brown, about 8–10 minutes. Add the cream and swirl off the heat until the caramel dissolves and the cream is light brown.
4. In a large bowl, add the caramel mixture and whisk together with the pumpkin, sugar, eggs, ginger and cream. Pour evenly into lightly oiled 4-ounce ramekins.

For the dessert course, Chef Brud created a deconstructed Pumpkin Pie with Cheddar Cheese crust, which is paired with Great Western Extra Dry Champagne. *Photo by Robyn Wishna.*

5. Place ramekins in a baking dish filled with 1 inch of hot water. Bake in a 325-degree oven for 25–30 minutes or until the filling is set and a toothpick inserted into the mixture comes out clean. Refrigerate until cold and firm.

6. For plating, run a sharp knife around the edge of the ramekin. Turn pumpkin filling onto a small dessert plate. Place crisp pastry pieces around the outside edge. Top with freshly whipped cream and a slice of aged cheddar cheese.

Chapter 4

THE EARLY 1900s

PROHIBITION AND ITS IMPACT IN THE FINGER LAKES

When learning about Reverend Bostwick's proactive approach to encouraging grape growing and winemaking in the Finger Lakes, one's immediate reaction might be to ask why a man of the cloth would promote the production and consumption of wine. The answer lies in understanding the context of the times. The early nineteenth century in the United States was a time of excessive over-drinking. We were, as Ken Burns noted in his 2011 documentary, "A Nation of Drunkards." An abundance of grain combined with the convenience and profitability of distillation resulted in a high number of stills (fourteen thousand of them in the United States in 1810) and an annual national per capita consumption of spirits of seven and a half gallons! Things were no different in the Finger Lakes. For example, the hamlet of Ithaca in 1816 was known as "Sin City" and "Sodom" and, according to an article in the local paper, was "notorious for its immorality. Horse-racing, gambling, sabbath-breaking, profanity, and intemperance were its crying sins."

In 1818, Thomas Jefferson, a huge vinophile[11] wrote: "No nation is drunken where wine is cheap, and none sober where the dearness of wine

---

11. A vinophile is a lover of wines.

substitutes ardent spirits as the common beverage. Wine brightens the life and thinking of anyone."

Reverend Bostwick took these words to heart. He and Deacon Samuel Warren believed that if they could help develop and promote a wine industry in the region that produced inexpensive but quality domestic wine, they could reduce their communities' harmful spirit-to-wine ratio as well as improve their economic well-being. This fell in line with the existing temperance movement in the 1830s, which was focused primarily on the abstinence of hard spirits. While their plan turned out to work extremely well, and the demand for Finger Lakes wine skyrocketed in the mid-1800s, there was a simultaneous shift in the beliefs of the temperance movement in the Finger Lakes. By the 1840s, the Washingtonian movement of temperance, which promoted total abstinence of all alcohol, took hold in the region. Nowhere in the region was the movement more pronounced than in Seneca Falls, located on the northern tip of Cayuga Lake. In 1842, the town of Seneca Falls voted to ban any consumption or sale of alcohol in its boundaries. It supported a temperance newspaper named the *Water Bucket*, which held the motto of "Total Abstinence from All That Can Intoxicate." The burgeoning Finger Lakes wine industry was lumped along with beer, cider and spirits as the source of the sins in their community. All throughout the region, farmers either volunteered or were pressured to cut down their apple trees and pull out their vineyards, or to return to selling their crop as fresh fruit and juice instead of fermented product.

In Seneca Falls, the temperance movement, led originally by Elizabeth Cady Stanton and Susan B. Anthony, soon became integrated into the larger faceted women's rights movement. Early feminists blamed alcohol on destroying families economically (by eroding household incomes on alcohol purchases and replacing men's work in the fields with drunken stupors), socially (by enticing men away from their homes and into the saloons) and medically (inebriated men making poor decisions would contract syphilis via their indiscretions). Without any legal standing for divorcing their drunk husbands or voting for protective laws, women began to organize to protect themselves and their families by demanding legal rights. It turned out, as stated quite eloquently by Finger Lakes writer Gary Cox, that "Susan B. Anthony, Elizabeth Cady Stanton and others in the Finger Lakes region played internationally important parts in what eventually proved to be a very powerful but unsustainable over-reaction to the drunkenness, mainly of men, in 19th-century America."

By January 1919, the Eighteenth Amendment prohibiting the manufacture, sale, transport, import or export of alcoholic beverages was the law of the land. The impact on the still young Finger Lakes wine industry was immediate.

The Wesleyan Chapel, originally built in 1843, was the site of First Women's Rights Convention. Today, it is part of the Women's Rights National Historic Park, a worthy stop on any trip to the Finger Lakes. *Public domain.*

Many small wineries closed down, but larger ones were allowed to stay open with special federal licenses for the making of wine for legal purposes. While total volume plummeted to a small fraction of its highest production levels, loop holes in the Volstead Act, which specified the details as to how the Eighteenth Amendment would be enforced, kept the six largest wineries of the region surviving through repeal in 1933. During Prohibition, Finger Lakes wineries could legally produce wine in the following ways:

- for sacramental wines
- for medical prescriptions written by doctors
- for sale to vinegar manufactures
- for sale to manufactures of wine "tonics" for medicinal use
- for use as a flavoring in prepared food or tobacco products
- for the production of brandy to be used in fortified sacramental wine

Since the Volstead Act had a provision allowing legal production of fruit juices in the home, some wineries also became very creative in finding ways

This letter was written by an Ohio resident to the Pleasant Valley Wine Company in 1921. The author had a rather loose interpretation of the Volstead Act's allowance of alcohol with a doctor's prescription. The letter reads: "Under the present ruling of the Federal authorities, wine is allowed to be sold for medical purposes. The doctor has recommended Champagne for me. Please let me know if you will ship some, and what price you have on Great Western Extra Dry." *Public domain.*

to fill the high demand of Americans seeking to make homemade wine. For example, concentrated "grape bricks" sold by a winery conglomerate in Penn Yan came packaged with yeast tablets and the following warning: "Warning. Do not place this brick in a one gallon crock, add sugar and

A stunning photograph of the 1921 harvest in the vineyards along Keuka Lake. *Courtesy of Bill Hecht.*

An ad for Taylor Wine Company's sparkling grape juice. Other unique products made from grapes that came out during Prohibition included grape ketchup, grape-flavored tobacco and grape fudge. *Photo by Laura Winter Falk.*

water, cover, and let stand for seven days or else an illegal alcoholic beverage will result."

Ironically, concentrated grape products, the most popular of which was called "Vine-Glo," along with a service to help initiate winemaking in the home, was supported by a grant to the grape growers under a federal farm relief program. In reality, the grape growers of the Finger Lakes managed to do pretty well during Prohibition, as public tastes and demand for fresh grapes and juice increased. It was believed that over 100 million gallons of wine was being made in the home, and while a vast quantity of grapes came from California, the American public loved "the pretty, big, round things that look as if they should yield good wine" coming from the Finger Lakes.

According to an article in *Fortune* magazine written in 1934, labrusca grapes from the Finger Lakes went from $12–$18 a ton before Prohibition to over $200 a ton in the New York market. Throughout Prohibition, 50 million baskets of fresh grapes left by railcar each year out of the region headed to cities around the northeast. Americans also discovered that the American varieties of grapes that grew throughout the Finger Lakes were ideal eating grapes as well. Eating fresh grapes was still a pretty novel concept in the world, and producing fresh grape juice by heating the freshly pressed grapes to thwart fermentation wasn't introduced until 1893. Liberty Hyde Bailey, founder and first dean of Cornell's College of Agriculture, wrote: "North America has given the world a new fruit in its grapes. This American grape is much unlike the European fruit. It is essentially a table fruit, whereas the other is a wine fruit."

While much attention was given to grape growing and its variations during this period, other significant events occurred that dramatically affected the region as an agricultural center. One aspect of the Finger Lakes that sets it apart from other agricultural regions in the country is its long relationship with Cornell University, New York State's land grant institution. As a land grant institution, Cornell is responsible for providing the dissemination of its agricultural research. In the early 1900s, Cornell added Home Economics to its extension services, responding to the importance of educating farm wives in issues related to home and family life, particularly in the area of health and child nutrition. The School of Home Economics at Cornell, championed by Martha Van Rensselaer, was founded on the belief that farmers' wives needed scientific training in order to carry out their roles as household managers. During the Prohibition years, Cornell released fifty-seven editions of the *Cornell Bulletin for Homemakers*, with topics such as "Food Preservation," "How to Use Apples as Food," "Milk as a Daily Food," "The Art of Vegetable Cookery," "Foods for Pre-School Children 2–6 Years of

Age" and "Low Cost Food for Health." These bulletins were designed to help the rural homemakers manage their households, maintain a healthy home and adjust to economic challenges that began to emerge particularly in the last years of Prohibition.

Recipe and Wine Pairing

I asked Cookie Wheeler, executive chef and general manager at Pumpkin Hill Bistro, on the east side of Cayuga Lake, to provide a recipe that depicts what people were eating during the era of Prohibition. I couldn't have chosen better. Cookie's grandparents were farmers, and she grew up spending weekends with them on the farm, where she learned the value of the dollar and working to raise what you eat, as well as how to turn all the farm's produce, dairy and meat into a meal that would not only fill the stomach but also warm the soul. This attitude permeates every inch of the farmhouse and twenty scenic acres that encompass Pumpkin Hill. When walking into the bistro, it feels like you are sitting down for a country meal with family and friends, and the locally sourced food and wine on Cookie's menu truly do fill your stomach and warm your soul.

Here is what Cookie had to say about her choice of recipe:

During this time period on the farm, it was a decade of cutting back and stretching what you had. Although there was an ample supply of low-end or cheaper cuts of meat available, the need to stretch those cuts to provide more meals was at the top of the homemaker's list. This brought about meals such as the beef loaf, or as it is more commonly known, meatloaf. Many processed food items were being introduced during this period, French's Worcestershire sauce being one of them. Wrapping the meatloaf in pastry topped with demi-glace is my way of modernizing it for today's palate while maintaining its comfort-food appeal.

I chose to pair Cookie's Meatloaf Wellington with Smokehouse Red from Standing Stone Vineyards. Standing Stone is located along the southeast shores of Seneca Lake, known as the "Banana Belt" due to its warmer microclimate. Owners Tom and Marti Macinski take advantage of their special *terroir* and grow Cabernet Sauvignon, one of the last vinifera

72

Chef Cookie Wheeler at Pumpkin Hill Bistro. In addition to serving up creative country fare, the bistro makes its own wine. *Photo by Laura Winter Falk.*

varietals to ripen for the season. The Smokehouse Red blend of Cabernet Sauvignon, Petite Verdot and Pinot Noir is the perfect complement to the rustic flavors of this classic meatloaf-with-a-twist recipe. I was first drawn to using Smokehouse Red for this era because of its namesake's story. The front of the bottle features an early 1930s photo of an old stone smokehouse on the vineyard property, a reminder of its earlier days as the Marsh family chicken farm. While a classic vinifera red, this wine is offered at a very affordable price, making it the perfect pairing in both representing the essence of the period and in its complementing flavor.

Cabernets are always a good choice with beef dishes. The tannins in the wine add structure that stands up to the stronger flavors of the meat, and the protein and fat in the beef softens these tannins to bring out a more velvety texture and enhance the fruit flavors in the wine. Some of the special ingredients in this recipe make the wine pairing experience even better. The wine enhances the flavors of the added vegetables. The flavor of the red peppers both in the recipe and as a garnish pop with the wine.

Cookie Wheeler's Meatloaf Wellington paired with Standing Stone Vineyards Smokehouse Red. *Photo by Robyn Wishna.*

The earthy and slightly sweet portobello mushrooms tossed with balsamic extend beautifully into the wine's finish. Lastly, the savory demi-glace sauce made from Cabernet Franc and the creamy texture and flavors of the pastry are completely unified by pairing it with a Cabernet-based wine.

MEATLOAF WELLINGTON
(paired with Standing Stone Smokehouse Red)

Serves 6

INGREDIENTS

½ cup diced white onions
½ cup diced mixed peppers (red and yellow)
3 tablespoons olive oil
1 tablespoon chopped garlic
¾ teaspoon thyme
1½ teaspoon oregano
1¼ pounds of ground pork
1¼ pound ground beef
¼ cup Worcestershire sauce
¼ cup ketchup (for a zestier version, substitute barbecue sauce)
1 teaspoon salt
½ teaspoon pepper
¾ cup panko crumbs (Japanese breadcrumbs or unseasoned breadcrumbs)
3 eggs
1 onion, sliced into strips
2 large portobello mushrooms, washed and sliced into strips
4 tablespoons butter
1 package puff pastry, thawed in refrigerator
1 egg and 2 tablespoons of water for an egg wash

PROCESS

1. Sauté onions and diced mixed peppers in the olive oil until the onions are translucent. Add garlic and sauté for approximately 3 minutes more. Set aside to cool.
2. In a large bowl, mix ground pork and beef until well combined. Add cooled onions, peppers and Worcestershire sauce, ketchup or

barbecue sauce, salt, pepper, panko crumbs and eggs and mix until well combined.

3. At this stage, you can either divide into 6 individual portions and place each portion in a jumbo muffin tin or form into a loaf.

4. Bake at 350 degrees until internal temperature reads 165 degrees (approximately 25 minutes for individual or 45 minutes for loaf). Set aside to cool.

5. Remove one sheet of the puff pastry and cut into 6 equal squares for individual wellingtons or uncut for an individual loaf. On a lightly floured surface, roll pastry until large enough to wrap around the meatloaf. Seal the edges and the outside of the puff pastry with egg wash. You may take the additional sheet and trim into strips to decorate the wellington if you like.

6. Bake at 375 degrees until golden brown.

7. Serve with smashed potatoes and finish with demi-glace.

DEMI-GLACE

INGREDIENTS

2 cups beef stock
1 cup red wine (Finger Lakes Cabernet Franc is perfect here)
2 tablespoons chopped shallot
2 teaspoons fresh chopped thyme (or ½ teaspoon dried)
1 bay leaf (optional)
pepper to taste
2 tablespoons butter

PROCESS

1. Place all ingredients except for butter in large sauté pan.

2. Cook at a medium simmer until the mixture reduces almost by half. Test the sauce's thickness by placing the back of a spoon into the sauce. If the sauce coats the spoon evenly, it's done.

3. Remove the sauce from the heat.

4. When ready to serve, stir in the butter until completely melted.

Chapter 5

POST-PROHIBITION

THE REBUILDING OF A DAMAGED INDUSTRY

By 1933, the "Noble Experiment" was over. The Twenty-first Amendment repealed Prohibition, and the Finger Lakes wine industry was again open for business. However, the damage from Prohibition was significant. Despite some wineries being able to keep their doors open, overall wine production in the United States dropped 94 percent from 1919 to 1925. Lost production was not the only casualty of Prohibition. Fourteen years of homemade wine and bootlegged spirits had changed American palates. In addition, the country was in the midst of the Great Depression, and Americans were unemployed and broke. Demand for high-quality champagnes were replaced with the desire for cheap blended "jug wine" and sweet, high-alcohol fortified wines like Richard's Wild Irish Rose[12] to numb the pain of the times.

The Finger Lakes wine industry had a lot of rebuilding to do. At first, it was believed that because of the quality wine coming out of the Finger Lakes prior to Prohibition, the region had the advantage of grabbing the

---

12. The success of Richard's Wild Irish Rose, one of the first branded wines in America, was so significant that it laid the financial foundation for Finger Lakes' Canandaigua Wine Company, later renamed Constellation Brands, which eventually became the largest wine company in the world.

revived American market. Following is a quote from an article written in *Fortune* magazine in 1934, only a few months after Prohibition was repealed: "But for all the people who have taken up the fad of wine drinking, New York offers the hope of a decent wine to drink. Champagne-making requires less of a grower's than a blender's skill, and the vintners of the Finger Lakes district have proved that they can practice it."

Unfortunately, the harsh reality of economics overruled the opportunity for the Finger Lakes to reemerge in the public eye as the region of quality in the domestic wine market. Of the more than fifty wineries that existed in the Finger Lakes prior to Prohibition, only four main wineries dominated.[13] Having to compete with California's growing control of vast quantities of grape and wine production, the region was forced into making wines as inexpensively as possible. Production exploded, but quality suffered. By the 1950s, the Finger Lakes was producing an estimated 100 million gallons of wine a year. Wines were still based on the native varieties that served as the foundation for their quality sparkling wines, but in order to drive the price down and decrease the wine's acidity to comply with American's tastes and wallets, they were often diluted with water. In addition, sugar was added, and cheap, neutral-flavored wine trucked in from California often composed up to 25 percent of the wine blend.

While business was booming, discontent with the quality of wine being produced in the region was brewing. A contingent of people believed that the Finger Lakes region was capable of making quality wine and that the American palate and wallet were ready for them. After the end of World War II, the country headed into what became the biggest economic boom it had ever experienced. The baby boom would result in the largest number of available wine consumers by the mid-1960s.[14] Men returning from Europe after the war had been introduced to the taste of finer quality wines while overseas and were looking for them back home. One of the first men to recognize the potential of better wine in the Finger Lakes was Charles Fournier. Mr. Fournier, who was a Frenchman, gave up a position at Veuve Cliquot Ponsadin, one of the most noted champagne houses in France, to

---

13. These four wineries—Taylor Wine Company, Pleasant Valley Wine Company (which merged with Taylor at the end of 1961), Widmer Wine Cellars and Gold Seal Vineyards—controlled the Finger Lakes wine industry and had the money and political influence over the next forty years to thwart all New York wine legislation that was not in their best interest.

14. From 1950 to 1980, per capita wine consumption doubled from one to two gallons per person.

In addition to offering wine tastings and tours of its historic facility, Pleasant Valley Wine Company has a wine museum with collectables dating back to the beginning of the winery. This collection of wine labels from the mid-1950s includes not only brands promoting native varietals like Niagara and Catawba but also those using familiar European wine regions and varietals such as Sauterne, Champagne, Gewurtztraminer and Chardonnay, most likely supplemented by wine from California. *Photo by Laura Winter Falk.*

run the newly restructured Gold Seal Winery. Arriving in 1934, he brought with him his own yeast culture as well as his expertise in producing world-class champagnes to revive the winery. By 1950, Gold Seal's reputation for French-styled champagnes was undeniable. At the 1950 California State Fair, Gold Seal brought home two medals out of the five distributed in the Sparkling Wine category. The following year, California closed its State Fair wine competition to out-of-state entries. Another huge success for Charles Fournier was his decision to produce a fruity rosé wine named Catawba Pink. This native-grape wine went on to become the bestselling wine at Gold Seal.

Charles Fournier's commitment to improving winemaking in the Finger Lakes was not limited to his work with the native labrusca grapes growing in the region. While working in France, he had become familiar with a new breed of grapes known as French-American hybrids. These grapes were genetic hybrids created in France by cross-pollinating American *Vitis labrusca*

79

Charles Fournier arrived in the Finger Lakes to rebuild Gold Seal Winery in 1934 and dedicated the rest of his life to developing the Finger Lakes wine industry. In 1982, eighty-one-year-old Fournier was named Man of the Year by California's *Vines and Wines* magazine. *Courtesy of Steuben County Historical Society.*

grape varieties with the European *Vitis vinifera* varieties.[15] These new grape varieties possessed the resistance to disease and harsh weather inherent in their labrusca ancestry and the less acidic, more complex flavors of their vinifera lineage. These French-American hybrids provided the Finger Lakes winemaker the foundation for making more interesting and subtle wines than was possible from the highly acidic and highly aromatic native grapes being used. Enthusiastic about the opportunity to create more complex wines, Fournier planted the earliest commercial vineyards of French-American hybrids in the United States in 1944. Following his lead, grape growers began pulling out their native vines and replacing them with the new hybrid varieties. In 1954, there were 35 acres of hybrid vineyards producing 104 tons of grapes in the Finger Lakes. By 1974, there were 2,500 acres producing 7,000 tons of hybrid grapes.[16]

No one in region was more dedicated to the idea that the future of Finger Lakes wine lay with the French-American hybrids than Walter S. Taylor. In the 1960s, while serving as assistant vice-president at his family's Taylor Wine Company, Walter Taylor was a highly vocal critic of the poor-quality wine being produced at the winery and throughout the region. He believed that the Finger Lakes could produce quality wine that consumers would love by using nothing but 100 percent Finger Lakes juice made from French-American

15. *Vinifera*, which translates from Latin as "wine-bearing," is the species of grapes that originated from Europe and is the basis of most commercial wine consumed today.

16. This information, as well as other detailed descriptions of the Finger Lakes wine history during the post-Prohibition years to the present day, is documented in a fabulous sourcebook titled *The Wines of the Eastern North America* by Hudson Cattell, who has been writing and promoting Finger Lakes and other eastern wine regions for almost forty years.

Walter S. Taylor with Hermann Wiemer at Bully Hill Vineyards. *Courtesy of Bully Hill Vineyards.*

hybrid grapes. In 1958, Taylor started Bully Hill Farms, converting the existing native grape vineyards on the property to French-American hybrids. After being fired from the Taylor Wine Company for his outspokenness, he opened Bully Hill Vineyards in 1970, establishing the first 100 percent estate-grown winery in the Keuka Lake area since Prohibition. Taylor was so committed to promoting local growing that the label of every bottle of Bully Hill wine sold listed each of the ingredients, as well as the local Finger Lakes growers from whom he purchased the grapes.

Supporting the grape growers and the development of hybrid varieties in the Finger Lakes was the New York State Agricultural Experiment Station (NYAES), located in Geneva, at the north end of Seneca Lake. Established in 1880 and part of Cornell University since 1923, the NYAES works "to safeguard New York's production of fruits and vegetables, develop new crops, enhance food safety for consumers, and promote economically viable farming solutions." The changing and expanding grape industry of the mid-century created interest in product improvement. The NYAES was

Clusters of Cayuga White grapes ready for harvesting. *Courtesy of Missouri State Fruit Experiment Station, Mountain Grove, Missouri.*

working diligently to raise the quality of wine made in the area by creating new hybrid varieties designed specifically to thrive in the Finger Lakes and New York State. One of its first and subsequently most successful varieties was the Cayuga White, which was first described in 1952 and first planted in 1964 in a formal trial that evaluated the most commercially promising French-American hybrid varieties. One of the three sites selected for the trial was the vineyard of Taylor Wine Company. The grape showed to be wonderfully suited for the region. Its vine was highly vigorous and was able to withstand temperatures as low as -20°F. Grape yield was very high with large fruit clusters and larger-than-medium berries. The resulting wine was described as a having a pleasant and delicate aroma, nicely balanced, fruity and European in style, resembling Riesling.[17]

Consumer response to the hybrid wines coming out of the Finger Lakes was significant. An article written by Tom Marvel in *Gourmet* magazine in 1957 elaborates: "Combining the delicacy of the European grape with the hardiness of the American vines, Franco-American hybrid grapevines presage a quiet revolution in Finger Lakes winemaking. They open new horizons for the American wine drinker and for our most promising eastern wine district."

While support was clearly growing for the French-American hybrids in the Finger Lakes, Charles Fournier's true dream was to grow and produce wines in the region using the European *Vitis vinifera* grapes, which undeniably made the highest-quality wine in the world. However, it had been long believed that vinifera could not grow in the region. As Charles Fournier described: "We had tried, with the able assistance of Philip Wagner of Maryland, but we had only been successful with small experimental vines that were brought indoors during the winter. The Geneva station had discouraged me from experimenting more because the winters are too harsh in New York."

Since colonial times, people searched for the way to grow *Vitis vinifera* in the Northeast. They thought the problem was the harsh weather. But there was one man who was not convinced. He was Dr. Konstantin Frank, an immigrant from the Ukraine. Dr. Frank held a PhD in viticulture and agronomy, specializing particularly in growing vinifera in cold-climate regions. Speaking no English, he came to the United States in 1951 at the age of fifty-two with the goal of proving that the noble winemaking grapes of Europe could be grown in the cool-climate Finger Lakes. He made his way to the Finger Lakes believing that if he could work with researchers at the NYAES, they could get vinifera to grow in the region. However, because the NYAES was very invested in its hybrid program at this time, it was not convinced that it should divert back to vinifera research after the original failings in large-scale commercial growing. Dr. Frank worked in blueberry research at the NYAES, and he grew further frustrated with not being able to present his ideas. This all changed when, at a seminar, he had the opportunity to talk with Charles Fournier. Fournier recalls the meeting:

---

17. A delicious sparkling wine made from 100 percent Cayuga White by Hosmer Winery is featured in the recipe pairing in chapter three of this book.

Charles Fournier (left) and Dr. Konstantin Frank (right), pictured here in the 1970s, helped set the course of reestablishing the Finger Lakes as a premier wine region in the second half of the twentieth century. *Courtesy of Dr. Konstantin Frank Vinifera Wine Cellars.*

I was attending a seminar at the experimental station in Geneva…I met a man in the hallway who was quite emphatic, and he said, "Why do you not grow Vitis vinifera *grapes in New York? This man insisted it could be done. He took me by the lapel and told me he had done it in Russia in a climate similar to New York's and that he could do it here. That man was Dr. Konstantin Frank.*

Dr. Frank acknowledged that the wine currently being made was good, but it was not the best. In Dr. Frank's own words, "Good grape varieties are not good enough for Americans. You Americans deserve only excellent."

Charles Fournier hired Dr. Frank as Gold Seal's director of research after that meeting, thus planting the seed for the next evolution of winemaking in the Finger Lakes.

RECIPE AND WINE PAIRING

It is worth noting that while wine was working its way into the social lives of Americans, the cocktail culture took off as a social phenomenon in the 1950s. The Cornell University Library's online exhibition Song of the Vine, which celebrates its Wine and Grape Archive, notes:

> *Cocktails, defined as "iced drinks of wine or distilled liquor mixed with flavoring ingredients," actually date back to the early 1800s when brandy, gin or rum was mixed with water, bitters, sugar or nutmeg. As America became increasingly prosperous, and as leisure time increased with the adoption of the standard eight-hour work day, the hour immediately after work became known as "cocktail hour," when people came together for good company, conversation and relaxation. Cocktail culture defined societal norms during the middle years of the 20th century. Americans created home bars, threw drinking parties and became fluent in the language of liquor.*

Chef Scott Signori of Stonecat Café, located along the east side of Seneca Lake in the town of Hector. *Courtesy of Scott Signori.*

I asked Scott Signori, owner and executive chef of Stonecat Café, to come up with both a food and cocktail recipe that evokes and celebrates mid-twentieth-century living in the Finger Lakes. Since 1999, Scott has been living in Hector on the east side of Seneca Lake, which he described in a 2012 *GQ* article as "a decidedly lawless community of redneck gourmets… so serious about their food, wine and music." Stonecat Café serves as the epicenter of this community movement by boldly declaring on its website that its mission is "to wake people up to life with dynamic, fun food and libation." Scott achieves this with his ever-changing seasonal menu featuring organic, locally sourced ingredients.

Here is what Scott had to say about his recipe selection:

My memory of Rumake stems from my mother's fancy cocktail parties in the late '60s and early '70s. My brother and I used to dip licked popsicle sticks into dry whiskey sour mix and steal Rumake from the kitchen in our PJs. My mother got the recipe from her mother, and of course, she has similar stories from her childhood in the 50's when kids were to be seen and not heard at cocktail parties.

RUMAKE
(paired with Six Mile Creek Winery Vignoles)

INGREDIENTS

½ cup tamari or soy sauce
¼ cup maple syrup plus 2 ounces
½ teaspoon sambal red chili paste
1 teaspoon chopped garlic
2 pounds chicken livers

2 (4-ounce) cans whole
    water chestnuts
2 pounds bacon
wooden sandwich picks

PROCESS

1. Mix together tamari, ¼ cup maple syrup, sambal and garlic.
2. Mix the remaining 2 ounces of maple syrup with 2 ounces of the marinade. Set aside for basting.
3. Put chicken livers and water chestnuts into liquid mix to marinate overnight.
4. Cut bacon in half.

Scott Signori's classic Rumake paired with Six Mile Creek Vineyard Vignoles. *Photo by Robyn Wishna.*

5. Fold water chestnut into chicken liver. Wrap bacon tightly around chicken liver.
6. Skewer with wooden sandwich pick, making sure to go through the end of the bacon.
7. Baste with reserved marinade and broil for 2–3 minutes on each side until bacon is cooked and caramelized.

In homage to this era of mid-century Finger Lakes, we have paired his fun appetizer in two ways: 1) with a Finger Lakes wine made from a classic French-American hybrid and 2) with Stonecat Café's interpretation of a classic cocktail.

The wine selected to pair with the Rumake was Vignoles from Six Mile Creek Winery. Six Mile Creek is owned by Roger and Nancy Batistella and located in Ithaca near the Cornell University campus. Not being able to take advantage of the lake's meso-climate, Six Mile Creek grows only white grapes in its vineyards, and Vignoles is one of its best. This highly expressive French-American hybrid wine is a wonderful combination of fruit and acidity. The flavor of pineapple abounds in this Vignoles, making it a perfect complement to the Rumake's teriyaki marinade. Also, the high acidity of the wine cuts beautifully into the fat and richness of the chicken liver and bacon, leaving a clean finish and tempting you to eat more.

In addition, every cocktail party has to have a great cocktail, and this one is it: Plum Sage Martini made with Finger Lakes Distilling McKenzie Distiller's Reserve Gin. This beverage represents Stonecat's Garden to Glass program of innovative cocktails created from herbs and produce sourced right from its organic kitchen garden and locally sourced spirits and juices. Here is how the bartending team at Stonecat describes it:

> At the Stonecat, we have been on the front line of what some have called a trend: using the freshest products from local farms, delivered daily. We don't see it as a trend. We see it as a return to Old World food values—growing and eating what you are able to grow in our own backyard, much as our grandparents did.
>
> We are fortunate to have access to the amazing products grown by local farmers. We also supplement the local bounty with an organic garden of our own. Those in restaurants and at home have evolved "farm to table" into what we now know as "garden to glass." Our bartenders at the Stonecat take great joy in picking from our garden daily to create the many seasonal simple syrups and liquor infusions that our bar is well known for. You may

see a fresh bouquet of spearmint, or maybe a bowl of fresh-picked berries on the bar to represent what is coming from the garden that day. We revel in the "oohs" and "ahhhs" as customers enjoy a cocktail featuring juice from locally grown beets or a simple syrup made from sweet, or even spicy, peppers. We love to watch as we deliver a Bloody Mary and see customers munch down a garnish of dilly beans or pickled green beans that we have picked and pickled right from our garden. The garden-to-glass movement transcends any particular time period, as people have been incorporating the bounty of their own garden into their everyday meals and cocktails since the beginning of recorded history.

Our passion for a local expression of flavor goes far beyond the kitchen, helping to create and influence a fun and dynamic cocktail menu. Each and every one of us has the opportunity to use and be proud of the bounty that is around us to shape what we eat and drink, whether that be out at the restaurant or comfortably at home.

PLUM SAGE MARTINI
(made with Finger Lakes Distilling McKenzie Distiller's Reserve Gin)

INGREDIENTS

¾ ounce homemade ginger simple syrup
7–10 garden-picked sage leaves
2 dashes Fee Brothers Plum Bitters (Rochester, New York)
¾ ounce fresh lemon juice
2 ounces McKenzie Distiller's Reserve Gin
1 egg white

PROCESS

1. In a shaker, muddle ginger syrup, sage and plum bitters.
2. Add lemon juice, gin and the egg white. DRY-shake vigorously.
3. Add ice and shake until tin is really cold.
4. Serve in a chilled martini glass garnished with a single sage leaf.

Stonecat Café's Sage Plum Martini made with Finger Lakes Distilling McKenzie Distiller's Reserve Gin is one of the restaurant's signature cocktails in its Garden to Glass program. *Photo by Robyn Wishna.*

GINGER SIMPLE SYRUP

INGREDIENTS

1 pound peeled raw ginger, finely chopped
4 quarts water
2.5 quarts granulated sugar

PROCESS

1. Add water and ginger in a saucepan. Bring to a boil and then simmer for 1 hour.
2. Stir in sugar on low heat. Put aside and cool.
3. Once cooled, use a fine mesh strainer to remove ginger and then cover and refrigerate. Shelf life of one week.

Chapter 6

THE LATE 1900s

THE EMERGENCE OF *VITIS VINIFERA* IN THE FINGER LAKES: A TIME FOR PLANTING AND REBIRTH

Dr. Frank worked for Gold Seal from 1954 to 1962. During this time, he set out to prove that *Vitis vinifera* could prosper in the region by experimenting with the grafting of vinifera vines onto North American rootstock to increase the cold-resistance of the plant as well as protect it against disease. Dr. Frank created approximately 250,000 hand-grafted cuttings in exhaustive combinations of twelve vinifera varieties and fifty-eight different North American rootstocks. He planted these in nine different soil conditions in order to determine what European varietal/ North American graft best strengthened the vines and produced the highest grape yields. By 1960, the first commercial vinifera wines were introduced at Gold Seal: Pinot Noir, Chardonnay and Johannesburg Riesling, proving, on a small scale, that noble vinifera wines could be produced in the Finger Lakes.

No longer interested in working for someone else, Dr. Frank left Gold Seal in 1962 to open his Vinifera Wine Cellars. Both the vineyards and the winery were located on Keuka Lake, not far from Gold Seal. A scientist first, Dr. Frank grafted thousands of vinifera varieties on the

Dr. Konstantin Frank was a tireless researcher, experimenting with numerous *Vitis vinifera* varietals and growing conditions to create world-class wines in the Finger Lakes. Today, grandson Fred Frank and great-granddaughter Meaghan Frank carry on the tradition of creating fine vinifera wines in the winery's fifth decade of winemaking in the region. *Courtesy of Dr. Konstantin Frank Vinifera Wine Cellars.*

eastern Canadian rootstock. He ended up grafting and planting over sixty varieties of vinifera grapes. The most successful varietals of his research showed to be Riesling, Chardonnay, Pinot Gris, Pinot Noir and Cabernet Sauvignon.

In time, the noble varieties thrived. He demonstrated that the greatest wine varieties in the world can be grown in the Finger Lakes with a combination of the right rootstock, grape variety, soil condition and microclimate. This was meticulous work that gave the Finger Lakes grape growers the information they needed to grow the best grapes, but not everyone was convinced that vinifera was the best solution for the region.

The 1960s in the Finger Lakes was fraught with battles among wine industry leaders concerning which grapes would be the future of Finger Lakes winemaking. Stakeholders were split into four groups:

1) Those who believed native varieties should remain the basis for Finger Lakes wines
2) Those who believed that native varieties should be blended with California wines for balance
3) Those who believed that hybrids should be the foundation for Finger Lakes wines
4) Those who believed that the region should be focusing primarily on producing wines from European vinifera

The most influential leaders in this debate were the four big wineries: Taylor Wine Company, Pleasant Valley Wine Company, Gold Seal and Widmer. They drove what was grown in the region because they were the sole customers of the grape growers. In a descriptive study performed in 1973 on Finger Lakes grape growing, it was reported that in 1964, 80 percent of grapes grown in the Finger Lakes were still native, 18 percent were hybrids and only 2 percent were vinifera. By the early 1970s, the percentage of hybrids produced in the region had grown, but vinifera still remained only a small fraction of what was grown even though American wine consumers were moving toward drier wines.[18] Year by year, as the big wineries began changing ownership from the original Finger Lakes pioneers to large beverage conglomerates like Coca-Cola and Seagram's, their investment in purchasing Finger Lakes–grown grapes was getting smaller and smaller while the amounts purchased and shipped from California was getting larger and larger. This resulted in a surplus of Finger Lakes grapes left to rot in grape growers' fields. Grape growers began to develop an interest in opening their own wineries to make use of their overstock of grapes, but the business environment in New York State was not friendly to the small winemaker. To open a commercial winery in the early 1970s required the payment of high annual license fees and taxes to the state; however, more critical was the barrier that wineries could only sell 5 percent of the wine they produced on premises, as most wine had to be sold to liquor stores, distributors or wholesalers at a fraction of the price they could get by selling directly to consumers. Pressure from an ailing grape-growing industry finally led to the passing of the New York State Farm Winery Act in 1976. A law aimed directly at helping the farmers, it gave them the opportunity to be independent from the whims of the large beverage company. It also gave them the opportunity to make and sell their own wine from their own grapes

---

18. This data was reported in a Cornell University master thesis written by Hal Harry Huffsmith.

The intimate size of many Finger Lakes farm wineries often provides wonderful opportunities to witness winemaking in action. Weekdays in September and October are the best times to visit the region and see (and sometimes participate in) the excitement of harvest. *Courtesy of Heron Hill Winery.*

on their own property and, most importantly, on their own terms. The Finger Lakes Farm Winery was born.

It wasn't easy at first. By the late 1970s, the demand for California Chardonnay and Cabernet skyrocketed after the famous 1976 "Judgment of Paris" wine competition, in which California wine defeated French wine in a blind taste test competition.[19] The American palate was now fully embracing the noble *Vitis vinifera* grapes, and most Finger Lakes growers were still harvesting Native American grapes for their new wines. Growers were now realizing that what Dr. Frank had said over twenty years ago was right: vinifera was the future of Finger Lakes wine. Fortunately, thanks to Dr. Frank, they knew what, how and where to plant. Native American vines were ripped up, and rows of newly grafted Riesling, Chardonnay, Pinot Noir and other varieties were

---

19. *Bottle Shock*, released in 2008, is a great movie that depicts the story behind the "Judgement of Paris."

The number of Riesling vineyards in the Finger Lakes has exploded in the twenty-first century. From 2006 to 2011, the total vineyard land grew by more than 50 percent. More than 80 percent of New York State's total Riesling vineyards are located in the Finger Lakes, and more vineyards are being planted yearly. *Courtesy of Heron Hill Winery.*

Opposite: The Ginny Lee Café at Wagner Vineyards was the vision of founder Bill Wagner, who believed that wine and food are meant to be enjoyed together. The restaurant is named after his granddaughter. *Photo by Laura Wagner Lee of Wagner Vineyards.*

planted along the shores of the deepest Finger Lakes, Seneca and Cayuga, to provide optimal climate protection. The learning curve was steep for many of these new winemakers (many of whom had never made wine before), and there was a lot of undrinkable wine flowing around the region during those early years. But shining through were some beautiful examples of Riesling. Of all the vinifera varieties, Riesling seemed to genuinely thrive in the region. Its vines loved the cooler climate, which was similar to its native land of Germany. Its roots dug deep into the mineral-rich shale and limestone soils created by the tropical seas millions of years ago that were later churned and spread along the glacier-carved lakes. The resulting wines had a unique balance of fruit, mineral and acid character that began to create the footprint of what Finger Lakes Riesling could be. During this time, there was one winemaker who wasn't surprised by Riesling's affinity for our region. Hermann Wiemer, who originally worked for Bully Hill making hybrid wines and was eventually fired by Walter S. Taylor for his constant urging to convert to vinifera, knew how similar the Finger Lakes conditions were to those of his hometown in the Mosel region of Germany. He steadily planted more and more Riesling during the '70s and '80s, when no one was really drinking it here in the United States. Wiemer perfected his style for a leaner, crisper, dryer Riesling than what was currently available. And in the words of New York wine writer Evan Dawson, his wine "became the standard for the Finger Lakes."

With the new farm wineries attracting visitors to the area, a demand for quality restaurants and eateries in the area increased. Enterprising wineries on each of the lakes began opening restaurants on their properties to provide hungry travelers a reprieve from their wine tasting. In the 1970s, Bully Hill on Keuka started with soup and sandwiches and quickly expanded its menu from there. Glenora Wine Cellars and Wagner Vineyards on Seneca Lake both added full-service restaurants adjacent to their tasting rooms. Laura Wagner Lee, whose father, Bill, founded Wagner Vineyards, describes how their restaurant came to be:

My father's philosophy had always been that wine and food are a natural and enjoyable combination. One of his original concepts for the winery was the addition of a restaurant where people could be introduced to how wines and food complement each other. The Ginny Lee Restaurant, named after my daughter (who is now the restaurant's manager), was a kitchen with a deck that had a tent over it when it first opened in 1983. In 1990, my brother, John Wagner, designed and built the current dining room with its cathedral ceilings and a stunning vista of the vineyard and Seneca Lake. The Ginny Lee has always featured Wagner wines, and in 1997, we added the Wagner Valley beers to the menu.

Later in the 1990s, Cayuga Lake entered the culinary scene with Knapp Winery's Vineyard Restaurant being the first on the Cayuga Wine Trail to provide quality winery dining on the west side of the lake.

RECIPE AND WINE PAIRING

To represent the Finger Lakes food scene during this era, I turned to the iconic Moosewood Restaurant in Ithaca. The Moosewood Collective (currently a group of nineteen owner/operators) opened their restaurant in 1973 in order "to live an alternative lifestyle and be our own boss." Today, after forty-plus years and counting, the restaurant can be considered the mecca of vegetarian culture, attracting visitors from all over the world. The Moosewood was one of the first vegetarian restaurants to show that vegetarian food can be both healthful and full of taste at the same time. The Moosewood is considered a "driving force behind creative vegetarian

The owner-operators of the Moosewood Collective. *Courtesy of the Moosewood Collective.*

cuisine" and was named by *Bon Appétit* magazine as one of the thirteen most influential restaurants of the twentieth century. Bringing this fame to the collective and its restaurant are their cookbooks. The Moosewood Collective has written and published thirteen cookbooks that celebrate the flavors and freshness of vegetarian cuisine. Their readers flock to Ithaca to sit at one of their rustic tables and enjoy the recipes they know and love as they were envisioned.

I wanted to feature a three-course meal from the Moosewood so that you can see the versatility of their recipes and experience how well they pair with Finger Lakes wines. I asked Wynnie Stein, one of the chef-owners from the Moosewood Collective, to choose three recipes that best represent the magic of the Moosewood Restaurant. Here is what she had to say about her choices:

> *As a longtime chef-owner at Moosewood with 40-plus years serving delicious, whole foods and writing about them in our award-winning cookbooks, we know one thing for sure: simple but vibrant, fresh ingredients are the stars of the show! I chose these recipes based on their being Moosewood Restaurant favorites that were developed early on but are still featured on our menus. I also chose them knowing that their flavors will shine alongside the excellent Finger Lakes wines that are paired with them.*

All the recipes below, as well as their introductions, are adapted from the Moosewood Collective's most recent recipe book, *Moosewood Restaurant Favorites* (St. Martin's Griffin, 2013), and are reprinted here with their permission.

AUTUMN SALAD PLATE
(paired with Long Point Winery Estate Chardonnay)

Description from the collective:

> *At the beginning of autumn, when the new crop of local winter squash comes in, roasted squash is often added to composed salads at Moosewood. The sugars in squash caramelize when roasted, yielding a crisp surface and a creamy, super-sweet under-layer. There are so many good varieties of squash to choose from for roasting. Some of our favorites include acorn, delicata, kuri, butternut, buttercup, and sweet dumpling. This autumn salad plate is accented by a delicious pear-and-thyme dressing. Red-skinned Bartlett pears are very pretty on this plate, and sweet and juicy, but use the best pears you have available.*

For the wine pairing, we featured Long Point Winery's Estate Chardonnay. Long Point Winery is owned by Gary and Rosemary Barletta and is located on the eastern shore of Cayuga Lake. Long Point's Estate Chardonnay is a lightly oaked wine that accentuates the lovely earthiness of this salad from the smoked cheddar and the roasted pumpkin seeds. Like many Finger Lakes Chardonnays, the oak does not overpower the wonderful fruit in the wine. This fruit blends beautifully with the caramelization and sweetness of the squash in the salad. The pear-thyme dressing pulls the pairing together, bringing out both the fresh thyme aromas and flavors in the wine as well as the flavor of pear, which is a classic characteristic of cool-climate Chardonnays.

Serves 4 as a main dish, 8 as a side dish
TIME: 45 minutes

TOPPINGS

About 2 pounds of winter squash with skin left on (see head note)
1 tablespoon olive oil or vegetable oil
¼ cup pepitas (pumpkin seeds)
4 ounces sharp smoked cheddar
2 ripe pears

Moosewood's Autumn Salad Plate with Pear-Thyme Dressing served with Long Point Winery Estate Chardonnay. *Photo by Robyn Wishna.*

1 tablespoon lemon juice
¼ cup dried cranberries
about 8 cups salad greens (arugula, spinach, lettuce, baby greens)
Pear Thyme Dressing (recipe included)

PROCESS:
1. Preheat the oven to 400 degrees. Lightly oil a baking sheet.
2. Scrub the winter squash and then peel it, or don't. Halve it through the stem end and scoop out the seeds. Cut the halves horizontally into ½-inch slices. Small squash give you nice crescents, but if the squash is large, cut the slices into halves or thirds. In a large bowl, toss the squash pieces with the oil. Lay the squash out on the baking sheet about ½ inch apart and sprinkle with salt. Bake until easily pierced with a fork, about 20 minutes. Remove from the oven and set aside to cool.
3. While the squash bakes, spread the pepitas on a small tray and, if they are not already salted, sprinkle with salt. Toast in the oven for about 5 minutes, until somewhat puffed and crunchy. Set aside to cool. Slice or cube the cheese. Quarter the pears lengthwise and remove the core. Slice thinly. To

keep the cut surfaces of the pears from turning brown, sprinkle them with lemon juice. Make the dressing.

4. On a large platter or individual plates, make a bed of the greens. Arrange the roasted squash, pear slices and cheddar on top. Drizzle on the dressing or pass it at the table and sprinkle with the pepitas and cranberries.

VARIATION
Gorgonzola, blue cheese and chèvre also are delicious on this salad plate.

PEAR-THYME DRESSING

The taste and color of the dressing varies depending on the flavor and color of the pear you use. A red-skinned pear will make a dressing with flecks of red. A green pear, especially if you use the lime juice variation, will give a lovely green hue.

Yields 1 generous cup
TIME: 10 minutes

INGREDIENTS

1 pear
2 teaspoons minced fresh thyme
2 tablespoons water
2 tablespoons cider vinegar
½ teaspoon salt

⅛ teaspoon black pepper
⅓ cup olive oil
1 teaspoon Dijon mustard (optional)
1 to 3 teaspoons honey or maple syrup
  (optional)

PROCESS

1. Core the pear and cut it into chunks—no need to peel it.
2. Put the pear, thyme, water, vinegar, salt and pepper into a blender and puree.
3. With the blender running, slowly pour in the olive oil.
4. Taste, and add mustard and honey or maple syrup if you like.

VARIATIONS
Use lime juice instead of cider vinegar.
Substitute an equal amount of tarragon for the thyme.

Greek Lemon-Mint Beans and Vegetables
(paired with Dr. Konstantin Frank Vinifera Wine Cellars Old Vine Pinot Noir)

From the collective:

Combining healthful beans and vegetables is now being touted as one of the most nutritious ways to eat. Created in the early days of our menu development, bean and vegetable stews have been mainstay signature dishes at Moosewood Restaurant. We always appreciated the inherent nutrition and fiber in these ingredients, but just as importantly, we like to showcase clean, simple flavors that are enhanced by adding fresh herbs.

The Dr. Frank Old Vine Pinot Noir was selected for this recipe to celebrate and honor the Frank family's four generations of winemaking in the Finger Lakes. This Pinot Noir is made from original vines planted by Dr. Frank in the 1960s. In the Finger Lakes, Pinot Noir is a light-bodied red wine that is highly versatile with food. The Dr. Frank Pinot Noir was paired with this dish because of its subtle, soft, earthy flavors. The lightness of the Pinot Noir dances with the individual flavors of the vegetables, which would easily get lost if consumed with a bigger wine. The Pinot loves the salt, mint, dill and red pepper flavors in the recipe and helps to show them off by enhancing their presence. Using a soft sheep's feta is preferred when pairing with the Pinot Noir, as a stronger, sharper version might overwhelm the beautiful, delicate flavors of this wine.

Serves 6–8
Yields 8 cups
TIME: 45 minutes

Ingredients

1½ cups chopped onions
2 cloves garlic, minced or pressed
1 teaspoon salt
2 tablespoons olive oil
2 cups diced carrots
1½ cups diced red or
   green bell peppers
2 cups diced zucchini
¼ teaspoon red pepper flakes

14-ounce can of artichoke hearts in
   brine, drained and chopped
15-ounce can of white beans, rinsed
   and drained (1½ cups)
15-ounce can of diced tomatoes, or 2
   cups diced fresh tomatoes
2 tablespoons minced fresh mint
1 tablespoon minced fresh dill
¼ cup lemon juice
salt and black pepper

This Moosewood recipe dates back to the restaurant's early years in the 1970s. The wine was produced from grapes planted by Dr. Frank back in the 1960s. Together, the Greek Lemon-Mint Beans and Vegetables served with Dr. Konstantin Frank Vinifera Wine Cellars Old Vine Pinot Noir is a classic pairing featuring the bounty of the Finger Lakes. *Photo by Robyn Wishna.*

Vintage and current bottles of Dr. Konstantin Frank's award-winning wines alongside a photograph at the winery of Konstantin Frank, with son Willy and grandson Fred. *Photo by Laura Winter Falk.*

PROCESS

1. In a large covered skillet or soup pot on medium-low heat, cook the onions, garlic and salt in the oil until the onions are translucent, about 10 minutes.
2. Add the carrots and bell peppers and continue to cook for about 3 minutes until the carrots begin to soften. Add the zucchini and red pepper flakes and cook for about 3 minutes.
3. Stir in the artichoke hearts, beans and tomatoes, cover and simmer until all the vegetables are tender but still brightly colored, about 10 minutes.
4. Stir in the fresh mint, dill and lemon juice and add salt and pepper to taste. You may like it with more mint and dill.

VARIATION
Use 2 teaspoons of dried mint instead of fresh. Add it when you add the red pepper flakes.

SERVING AND MENU IDEAS
Serve on a bed of orzo, couscous or rice topped with a soft feta cheese or chèvre.

SARA'S FRESH APPLE-SPICE CAKE
(paired with Red Newt Cellars Lahoma Vineyards Riesling)

From the collective:

> *From the beginning in the early '70s, Moosewood Restaurant's cooks adapted family recipes to feature in the restaurant. That was the wellspring for creating a variety of ethnic and American regional favorites. Sara Robbins started at Moosewood in 1973 as a baker and dessert maker and shared a beloved family recipe from her talented Aunt Minnie of Atlanta, Georgia. This moist cake, a favorite of the South, is also perfect for upstate New York, a leading grower of apples of every variety.*

We paired this spice cake with the sweet Red Newt Cellars Lahoma Vineyards Riesling. Red Newt Cellars is owned by Dave Whiting and is located on the southeast shores of Seneca Lake. The Lahoma Riesing has a classic Riesling aroma and flavor of sweet peaches with a clean, almost effervescent acidic finish of pink grapefruit. When paired with the cake, there is a flavor explosion of nuttiness and baking spice, with sesame on the finish. The subtle sweetness of the cake does not overwhelm the wine. This allows the vibrant flavors of the wine to shine through without destroying its wonderfully crisp ending.

Serves 10–12
Yields one 10-inch Bundt cake or a 9- x 13-inch sheet cake
PREP TIME: 30 minutes
BAKING TIME: about 1 hour

INGREDIENTS

1¼ cups vegetable oil
2 cups brown sugar, lightly packed
3 large eggs
2 teaspoons vanilla extract
3 cups unbleached white all-purpose flour, or 2 cups white and 1 cup whole
   wheat flour
1 teaspoon baking powder
1 teaspoon baking soda
½ teaspoon salt

Sara's Fresh Apple-Spice Cake, a staple at the Moosewood Restaurant, paired with Red Newt Cellars Lahoma Vineyards Riesling. *Photo by Robyn Wishna.*

2 teaspoons cinnamon

½ teaspoon ground cardamom

3 tablespoons apple juice or cider, milk, buttermilk or water

3 cups chopped apples (peeled or not)

1 cup chopped walnuts or pecans (optional)

PROCESS

1. Butter or oil a 10-inch Bundt pan or a 9- x 13-inch baking pan. Either dust with flour or sprinkle with sesame seeds. Preheat the oven to 350 degrees.

2. In a large bowl, beat the oil and brown sugar for a couple minutes. Add the eggs one at a time, beating after each addition, and then beat until creamy. Beat in the vanilla.

3. In a separate bowl, sift together the flour, baking powder, baking soda, salt, cinnamon and cardamom. Add to the sugar-egg mixture along with the liquid, and beat until smooth. Fold the apples into the batter. Fold in the nuts, if using.

4. Pour the batter into the prepared pan and bake for an hour or more, until golden brown, fragrant, pulling away from the sides of the pan and firm to the touch.

5. If you made a Bundt cake, cool it in the pan for 10 or 15 minutes and then invert onto a serving plate. Serve sheet cake from the pan. Serve warm or at room temperature.

SERVING IDEAS

Plain, this cake is good for brunch or a snack. We usually dust it with confectioners' sugar after it has cooled. For dessert, it sure is good with whipped cream or ice cream.

Chapter 7

TODAY AND BEYOND

WORLD-CLASS RIESLINGS AND A LOCAVORE'S PARADISE

Coming full circle with it's beginnings in the 1860s, the Finger Lakes wine region is once again internationally recognized for producing world-class wines that have commanded long-awaited and resisted attention. Riesling has been the variety to bust open the gate, as described by wine writer Thomas Pellechia: "From New York City to Napa Valley, from Britain to Belgium, from the Rhine to the Rhone—Finger Lakes Riesling wines are considered world-class. Every local winemaker agrees that Riesling's future is solidified and unlimited." The *Atlantic* correspondent Caroline Helper notes, "At a time when the local food movement has inspired many consumers across the nation to, for the first time, consider the wines being made in their own backyards, no up-and-coming domestic region has received as much serious attention as the Finger Lakes of upstate New York. To be specific, it is the Rieslings of the Finger Lakes that have generated the most buzz."

But while undisputedly the queen grape of the region, Riesling is not the only wine getting attention. The Finger Lakes is recognized as one of the most diverse wine regions in the world. Today, hundreds of wineries are creating wines in the region, and the numbers have been changing exponentially with

Hand-harvesting delicate *Vitis vinifera*. *Photo by Nicole Young, courtesy of Dr. Konstantin Frank Vinifera Wine Cellars.*

50 percent of the wineries having opened since 2000. The New York Wine and Grape Foundation has reported that over nine thousand acres of Finger Lakes vineyards are producing seven major varieties of native labrusca, eighteen major varieties of European-American hybrids and at least nine major vinifera varieties. New varieties are continually being introduced in the vineyards for those still searching for the "next big wine" of the Finger Lakes. In 2013, the New York State Agricultural and Experiment Station, still the Finger Lakes vineyardist's best friend, released two new hybrid grape varieties ready for commercialization: the red Arandell and the white Aromella. Both varieties are cold tolerant and disease resistant with wonderful aromatics and fruit flavors. New European vinifera are also being planted in the region by those vineyardists who, following the path laid by Dr. Frank over fifty years ago, search for the perfect combination of *terroir*, rootstock and varietal in hopes of unveiling another grape that is as happy in our climate and as expressive in the glass as the Riesling. Cool-climate white vinifera such as Gewurtztraminer, Pinot Gris and Gruner Veltliner (an eastern European grape) and red varietals such as Teroldego (a grape from northern Italy), Lemberger (or Blau Frankish, as it is known in its native Austria) and Saparavi (from the former Soviet republic of Georgia) are all showing great aromas, flavors and promise.

James Molesworth, senior editor of *Wine Spectator* magazine, one of the most respected and cited wine magazines in the world, sums it up beautifully at the end of his first formal tasting report done on the Finger Lakes in February, 2013: "As the region's steadily growing ranks of winemakers gain experience, honing in on the best grapes and vineyard sites, the Finger Lakes is quickly becoming an excellent source for quality and value. It's time for serious wine consumers to take notice."

Despite exponential growth in the twenty-first century, the Finger Lakes is still a very small wine region on the world scale. In 2013, according to the New York Wine and Grape Foundation, the Finger Lakes produced 55,000 tons of grapes, while, according to the 2013 NASS crush report, California produced 4.8 million tons. The region produces less than 3 percent of American wine and less than a tenth of a percent of the world's wine. So to truly appreciate Finger Lakes wine, you must experience it firsthand at the wineries. The vast majority of Finger Lakes wine is sold directly from winery tasting rooms. To taste the wines where it is produced, among the glacial-sculpted hillsides and the long, narrow, deep blue lakes, is to appreciate the *terroir* that created it. The Finger Lakes is one of the most accessible wine regions in the world. Many of the winemakers throughout the region are the ones behind the bar, pouring your wines and sharing with you the story of the vintage. Opportunities exist at many of the wineries to tour the vineyards and the wine cellars and learn the painstaking but passionate work that went into creating the luscious wines you are drinking. On a weekday afternoon, you might run into the winemaker who has brought barrel or tank samples in the tasting room for the staff, or any lucky visitor who happens to be there, to taste and give him or her their opinions. This is when the Finger Lakes wine experience is at its best. The Finger Lakes wine region is more accessible to visitors today than it has ever been in its 150-plus-year history. There are four major wine trails that wind around the largest wine-producing lakes: Seneca, Cayuga, Keuka and Canandaigua. Along with their stunning lakeside views and endless opportunities to taste quality wine, the success of the region as a destination has led to new craft beverage producers to emerge. Throughout the Finger Lakes, you can experience top-quality farm distilleries, producing clear and barrel-aged spirits and fruit-based liqueurs all based on locally grown ingredients. The same is true for craft breweries, which have organized into the very popular Finger Lakes Beer Trail, where the flavors and creativity are as fresh as the hops fields growing right outside the tasting rooms. Lastly, craft cideries that incorporate our region's heritage and appreciation for the apple create a range of hard ciders, some of which incorporate the same heirloom apples used by those first European homesteaders in the 1700s. For example, Bellwether Hard Cider's King Baldwin is a blend of two eighteenth-century apples: the Tompkins King, an apple variety originating in Tompkins County, right here in the Finger Lakes, and the Baldwin, first discovered in 1740 in Massachusetts.

But the story doesn't end there. In fact, that is only half of it because alongside the explosion in quality beverage production is a region blossoming as a destination being recognized for what it has always done well: producing quality food from the gifts of the land. All around the country, Americans are embracing a farm-to-table culture, and nowhere is this booming more than in the Finger Lakes, where access and appreciation of the regional grower has always been paramount.

Here is some data that illustrates the importance agriculture still plays in the region in the twenty-first century. In 2007, according to the New York State Comptroller's Report, the Finger Lakes made $1.2 billion in agriculture sales from its 6,417 farms and 1.5 million acres of farmland. Various Finger Lakes counties led the state in production in milk and other dairy, tree nuts, berries, melons, potatoes and sweet potatoes. The apple is still king in the

Experience! The Finger Lakes' guests enjoying time during harvest in the Gewurtztraminer vineyards at Standing Stone Vineyards on Seneca Lake. *Courtesy of Experience! The Finger Lakes.*

Above: This gorgeous bleu cheese is created by Lively Run Goat Dairy in Interlaken. Lively Run is one of the longest-operating commercial goat dairies in the United States, producing artisanal goat cheese since 1982. Today, it produces over thirteen varieties of goat cheese from creamy fresh chèvre to the aged and nutty Finger Lakes Gold. It is also producing raw cow's milk cheeses such as this bleu, as well as gouda and cheddar. *Courtesy of Lively Run Goat Dairy.*

Opposite, top: Finger Lakes Distilling, on the east shore of Seneca Lake, is one of a number of farm distilleries in the Finger Lakes that have opened their doors since the passing of the Farm Distillery Act in 2007. Similar to the farm wineries, farm distilleries can produce their spirits and sell them directly to consumers in tasting rooms in New York State as long as New York farm and food products are used as ingredients and total annual production is under thirty-five thousand gallons. *Courtesy of Finger Lakes Distilling.*

Opposite, bottom: Hopshire Farm and Brewery, located in Freeville, just outside Ithaca, is a brewery committed to creating craft beers featuring New York State hops and other local agricultural products around the region. Rows of organic hops grow in the hopyards located right outside the entrance to the brewery. *Courtesy of Hopshire Farm and Brewery.*

Finger Lakes, which led in total state production and came in second in the entire nation in 2012.[20]

Another very exciting movement in the Finger Lakes since the early 2000s is the rise of artisanal cheese production. Artisan cheese-making has been a wonderful way for regional dairy farmers to go from selling a commodity milk product to a value-added product, increasing their earning potential. For example, in 2013, the commodity price of milk was around $19 per one hundred pounds of fluid milk. Used in cheese, that same one hundred pounds of fluid milk can make ten pounds of artisan cheese.[21] Here in the Finger Lakes, artisanal cheese retails for around $15–$20 per pound. So, for that same one hundred pounds of milk, the dairy farmer earns, on average, $180 rather than $19! Finger Lakes cheese-maker Keeley McGarr O'Brien, who has been making her artisan Irish-styled washed-rind cheese at her family's dairy farm since 2009, has this to say about the impact her cheese-making has had on her family's farm:

> *I feel strongly that there is potential, and great benefit, of value-added dairy. I'd also say that after only four years, we aren't there yet. There is a certain volume of production and sales we need to achieve in order to say we are playing a role in keeping the farm in business. But I am optimistic we could be there within the next five years. It's not a way to make a quick buck, that's for sure. There is a large amount of investment in knowledge and facilities/equipment. But if you're ready to make the investment, I think the more milk we can devote to our own value-added production, the better off we will be. I have seen the cyclical milk cycle take it's toll on small and medium-sized farms my whole life. Farming is a tough enough way to make a living; trying to hedge against ever-decreasing profit margins makes it almost impossible. One of my father's favorite quotes about farming was one made by JFK: "The farmer is the only man in our economy who buys everything at retail, sells everything at wholesale and pays the freight both ways." If we can make ourselves price makers (with our cheese), rather than price takers (selling fluid milk to a large co-op where we compete with farms many times our size),*

---

20. Some of the counties that are geographically in and, for the purposes of this book, considered part of the Finger Lakes are actually included in different New York State economic zones (examples include Tompkins, Cayuga and Schuyler Counties). Therefore, their figures are not included in these totals.

21. For soft cheeses, one may need only eight pounds of milk to make a pound of cheese, and for harder, aged cheeses, the number could be up to eleven pounds per pound of milk. But the general rule of thumb is ten to one.

Keeley McGarr O'Brien standing with one of the McGarr Farm calves. Keeley is part of the new generation of Finger Lakes farmers who are contributing to the success of their family's dairy farms by creating value-added artisanal cheese. *Courtesy of Keeley O'Brien of Keeley's Cheese Co.*

A typical weekend day at the Ithaca Farmers' Market at Steamboat Landing—the place to shop local, eat great food, taste wines and even take a narrated boat cruise on Cayuga Lake. At the end of the season in November, the annual rutabaga curl is not to be missed! *Courtesy of the Ithaca Convention and Visitors Bureau.*

Weekly fresh produce awaits those who purchase a share in a local CSA. *Photo by Laura Gallup, courtesy of Silver Queen Farm.*

Family farms like Silver Queen thrive throughout the Finger Lakes region. Locals and visitors alike can get direct access to farm-fresh food throughout the season through CSAs, farmers' markets, u-pick stands and local grocery stores. *Photo by Laura Gallup, courtesy of Silver Queen Farm.*

we are setting ourselves up for a truly sustainable business—one that can confidently be passed on to future generations. We're certainly lucky to be attempting this business model at a time when consumers are increasingly demanding local food and want to know the story behind that food.

In response to the increased demand for local foods, scores of farmers' markets exist throughout the Finger Lakes from Skaneateles to the east and Canandaigua to the west, with many in between in towns both big and small. The most lauded farmers' market in the region is the Ithaca Farmers' Market, which first opened to the public in 1973 as an innovative way for a handful of local farmers, craftspeople and food vendors to sell their goods directly to the eager Ithaca consumers. Today, with its 160 local vendors who sell everything from produce to freshly prepared ethnic food, baked goods, cheese, handcrafted artisan gifts, wine and flowers, it has been recognized by Zagat as one of the eight must-see farmers' markets in the United States—and the only one on the list not located a large metropolitan city.

Farmers' markets are just one of several ways in which farmers and growers of the region connect with eager (and hungry) consumers. CSAs (community-supported agriculture programs) abound throughout the region. CSAs provide a way for individuals and families to buy shares of a farm's seasonal bounty directly from the farmer. They pay money up front at the beginning of the season, which helps provide the farmer with the cash he or she needs to prepare and maintain the farm throughout the growing months. In return, the consumer gets fresh-off-the-farm and, often, organic produce (and meats if you have a meat CSA) each week that corresponds with what is being harvested. From crisp asparagus in May to pick-your-own berries throughout the summer and leafy greens and root vegetables into November, one picks up his or her weekly supply of Finger Lakes heaven. In 2013, about 4,500 shares, equal to approximately $2.25 million, in Tompkins County alone was spent and kept in the local economy through the CSA system.

More and more farmers in the Finger Lakes also are finding that agritourism is a way to educate people on the value of farming, as well as bring additional sources of income into the farm. The Finger Lakes has over 150 u-pick farms throughout fourteen counties selling everything from apples, grapes and berries to beans, tomatoes and pumpkins. Throughout the summer and into harvest, wine dinners on the farm give local chefs the opportunity to share the season's fresh bounty with guests in a beautiful natural setting. One Finger Lakes farm truly embracing agritourism is Silver Queen Farm. Gordie Gallup and his wife, Liz, started Silver Queen Farm in Trumansburg in 2001. They find themselves regularly engaging with visitors on the farm through their u-pick program; CSA; in the event barn that Gordie built, where they host farm dinners; fundraising galas; and weddings for up to two hundred guests! Gordie describes what inspired him to start farming in the Finger Lakes, as well as what attracted him to agritourism:

> *I was brought up on a farm and spent most of my youth working on farms. Given the nature of farming 30 years ago, I couldn't find a way to afford the financial investment it took to become a farmer…So I actually started in the Finger Lakes as a custom homebuilder, but the lure of farming in this magnificent area led me to invest every dime I made into starting a farm. My love of farming convinced me that sharing the love and beauty of growing good food should be an intricate part of our business. I love being a grower, but I also love sharing and educating others about the amazing world of farming. There is no greater joy than seeing someone learn and*

enjoy the wonders of farming. Things that we could easily take for granted are brand new and exciting to someone who is just learning about where and how their food is grown. With agritourism, this excitement is a constant reminder of how blessed we are to farm in the Finger Lakes.

At the top of the farm-to-table food chain is the extensive regional embrace of restaurants using locally sourced ingredients and beverages on their menus. In the mid-2000s, the region began to explode with farm-to-table restaurants featuring the local meat, produce, cheese, wine and other artisan beverages of the region. Jocelyn Zuckerman, who spent summers growing up in the Finger Lakes, is the author of a beautifully written article for *Gourmet* magazine from 2005 that recognized this new emergence as "pastoral pleasures of the Finger Lakes hiding in plain sight, somewhere between the vineyards and a new crop of farm-friendly restaurants."

Each major lake in the Finger Lakes has its top restaurants that showcase the best ingredients the region has to offer. On Keuka Lake, John and Jo Engel opened the Blue Heron Café at Heron Hill Winery in 2000. Esparanza Mansion at the top of Keuka has a farm-to-bar menu featuring locally grown herbs and spices in its mixed drinks. The west side of the Cayuga Lake Wine Trail is booming with dining choices at the wineries with the Copper Oven at Cayuga Ridge, the Vineyard Restaurant at Knapp Winery, the Crystal Lake Café at Americana Vineyards and the Bistro at Thirsty Owl Wine Company— all of which use their unique culinary perspectives to show off the fresh local products of our region along with their wines. In southern Cayuga, restaurants showing their commitment to local growers include the Hazelnut Kitchen and Creekside Café in Trumansburg and scores of Ithaca restaurants, showcased by Coltivare, the downtown Ithaca culinary center associated with Tompkins Cortland Community College's Farm-to-Bistro initiative. In addition to being a full restaurant, Coltivare includes learning labs, a demonstration kitchen and wine-tasting room. The restaurant's produce comes from the program's sustainable farming branch. The menu is brought to life by the culinary arts and wine marketing branches of the college. The initiative is one of a handful of educational programs in the country wherein students experience all parts of the culinary trade in one degree. Along with Coltivare, Agava, The Bistro at La Tourelle, the Bandwagon Brew Pub and Northstar House (just to name a few) celebrate Ithaca's incredible access to farm-fresh ingredients. In fact, there are so many options in Ithaca and Tompkins County that the area has its own website, Farm to Fork (www.ithacafork.com), that provides lists of the restaurants, farms and markets committed to locavore living.

Heron Hill Winery's tasting room on the west side of Keuka Lake was chosen by *Travel and Leisure* as one of the ten most spectacular tasting rooms in the world. *Photo by Stu Gallagher, courtesy of Heron Hill Winery.*

The restaurant at Elderberry Pond is nestled in a wooded lot within the one-hundred-acre farm that provides it with daily organically grown produce, flowers, herbs and pasture-raised meats. *Courtesy of Elderberry Pond Farm and Restaurant.*

On east Cayuga Lake, Pumpkin Hill Bistro and the restaurant at the Aurora Inn, both in the village of Aurora, and Elderberry Pond in Auburn create delicious seasonal menus based on local ingredients and local wines. Elderberry Pond restaurant takes the farm-to-table concept to the next level by sourcing its menu with ingredients from its thirty-five-acre certified organic farm. A meal at Elderberry Pond restaurant could include fresh-cut flowers from the garden at the table and dishes based on the herbs, fruits, vegetables, pasture-raised pork and grains all grown on its farm using 100 percent organic and sustainable practices. In the village of Skaneateles, at the northern tip of the eastern Finger Lake bearing the same name, the restaurant at Mirbeau Inn and Spa shows off its farm-to-table commitment within its French-inspired cuisine. The Sherwood Inn, a historic inn and restaurant in the heart of the village, boasts over fifteen Finger Lakes wines on its award-winning wine list that accompanies its classic American fare. In the western Finger Lakes, Canandaigua Lake shines its locavore beacon with the New York Wine and Culinary Center in the city of Canandaigua. The center is a celebration of everything New York, featuring a tasting room, culinary classes, hands-on cooking classes and the Upstairs Bistro, which serves locally sourced food, wine and beer. Also worth noting along southwest Canandaigua Lake is the tiny Brown Hound Bistro. Here the chef, in addition to sourcing his ingredients from local farmers, will head out into the surrounding forests with his staff and forage for edible delicacies like ramps, fiddleheads, cattail stalks and yarrow, which are then incorporated into the bistro's menu.

It is not surprising that Seneca Lake, being the largest of the lakes and with the largest number of wineries surrounding it, also has a large number of restaurants committed to farm-to-table cuisine. On the west side of Seneca, Verasions at Glenora Wine Cellars has focused its menu on seasonal ingredients sourced from local growers since 2005. From the Wildflower Café and Nickels Pit BBQ, featuring home-brewed beers and local wines in Watkins Glen, to the Red Dove Tavern and Ports Cafe in Geneva, appreciation and commitment to the local bounty is obvious. But on the eastern shore of Seneca Lake, locavores dine in delight. The aforementioned Stonecat Café, Dano's Heuriger, Red Newt Bistro and Suzanne Fine Regional Cuisine, some of the finest restaurants in the region, are separated by seven miles but united by the passion for quality food and wine. Among these four restaurants are two semifinalists for the James Beard award for Best Chef Northeast (Dano Hutnik and Suzanne Stack) and two pioneers of the local food movement in the Finger Lakes. In 1999, both Stonecat Café and Red Newt Bistro opened

Courtesy of www.visitfingerlakes.com.

their doors committed to showcasing the bounty of the region. Debra Whiting, co-founder of Red Newt with her husband Dave Whiting, was a visionary chef in the Finger Lakes region. From the bistro's inception, the focus has always centered on using local products purchased directly from local farmers and listing them on the menus—long before it became a national trend and long before "local" became an effective marketing term. As indicated on the Debra Whiting Foundation website, Debra's "passion was not just the food as it appeared on the plate, but the food as it grew on local farms, supported local farmers and communities, and offered a wholesome and rewarding lifestyle to an entire region." This foundation in her name supports events and scholarships that support "the spirit of farm-to-table." Today, Dave Whiting continues that tradition at Red Newt Bistro, creating creative local cuisine honoring the roots laid by Debra.

The literal grassroots ethos that thrives in this region is championed by the Finger Lakes Culinary Bounty, a regional food network whose members include growers, manufacturers, retailers, marketers, distributors and restauranteurs. Since 1999, members have worked together to facilitate and promote local eating and drinking. It is just one of the many organizations throughout the region that have helped to create the infrastructure that defines the Finger Lakes' culinary culture. An infrastructure established over a century ago with the region's close connections to cutting-edge agricultural research and support via the Cornell Cooperative Extension and the NYSAES. An infrastructure continually bolstered with cutting-edge, degree-bearing curricula at Cornell University and Finger Lakes Community College in enology and viticulture, and in the culinary arts and sustainable farming and food systems program at Tompkins Cortland Community College. An infrastructure enhanced when businesses like Regional Access create systemic links that bring the products of the Finger Lakes growers directly to retailers, restaurants and consumers. An infrastructure broadened when marketing associations like the beverage trails bring independent businesses together with the shared understanding that success as a whole is much greater than the sum of each of their individual successes. An infrastructure celebrated when fabulous local publications like *Edible Finger Lakes* magazine present in glorious color and print the special people and businesses that define the food and wine of our region. Together, these demonstrate that our rich culinary culture is not a passing fad; this is who we are. We are a region that has appreciated, celebrated and flourished with the natural gifts given to us. From the first Native American settlers to today, this defining cultural attitude continues, and it will be passed down to future generations to come. The rest of the world is starting to take notice of what we have been doing here all along, which is all very exciting but also, to those living here, just another day in the Finger Lakes.

RECIPE AND WINE PAIRING

Representing farm-to-table cuisine crafted at the most elegant level in the region is Suzanne Stack of Suzanne Fine Regional Cuisine. Suzanne and her husband, Bob, opened Suzanne FRC in 2003 after falling in love with the 1903 farmhouse overlooking Seneca Lake in the town of Lodi that serves as their home and restaurant. Suzanne's passion for fresh food drives every decision she makes in her kitchen. From spring asparagus until late autumn beets, Suzanne's master gardener works all season long in their one-hundred-acre garden nurturing the beautiful produce that serves as the basis of her meals. Suzanne sources her meats, cheese, eggs and other key ingredients from hand-selected local farmers, and the menu is paired with a wine list made

Suzanne Stack of Suzanne Fine Regional Cuisine in the kitchen of her restaurant, a 1903 farmhouse in Lodi with a breathtaking view of Seneca Lake. *Courtesy of Suzanne Fine Regional Cuisine.*

Suzanne's Beet Tower paired with Silver Thread Vineyard Gewurtztraminer. *Photo by Robyn Wishna.*

up entirely of Finger Lakes wines. The accolades bestowed upon Suzanne and the restaurant are both extensive and impressive. They included being named one of Frommer's Ten Best Places to Dine in New York State and the New York Wine and Grape Foundation's 2011 Restaurant of the Year, as well as winning *Wine Spectator*'s Award of Excellence multiple years running. Arguably most significant is Suzanne's recognition as a semifinalist for the James Beard award for Best Chef Northeast. But what drives Suzanne are not these awards, but her love of food and cooking, which shows with every plate served.

I asked Suzanne to create a full three-course menu, which we paired with three beautiful Finger Lakes wines. Suzanne describes her menu as one "that was designed with summer entertaining—sitting out in your gardens and enjoying a beautiful sunset. It's also a menu designed for all that our local markets have to offer." She reflects on her favorite aspects of each recipe, as well as its significance in representing her farm-to-table approach when creating her exquisite regional cuisine.

BEET TOWER
(paired with Silver Thread Vineyard Gewurtztraminer)

Layers of roasted beets and chive goat cheese spread dressed in a sherry vinaigrette served with candied walnuts, orange segments, a fresh herb mixture and micro-greens.

Bob Stack, who manages the wine list at Suzanne FRC, recommended that we pair the beet tower with a Finger Lakes Gewurtztraminer. I chose the Gewurtztraminer from Silver Thread Vineyard, which also resides on the east side of Seneca Lake, less than three miles from the restaurant. Silver Thread Vineyard is owned by Paul and Shannon Brock, who represent the next generation of winemakers in the Finger Lakes. Gewurtztraminer is known for its combination of floral aromas, fruit and spice. Silver Thread's version of Gewurtztraminer delivers on those characteristics and then some. There is a beautiful citrus quality to this wine that pairs perfectly with the orange segments and vinaigrette, while at the same time accentuating the sweetness of the beets, the herbaceous and savory richness of the chive goat cheese and the sweet nuttiness of the candied walnuts. This is a complex wine that dances effortlessly with the myriad flavors in this elegant starter.

Here is what Suzanne had to say about her recipe:

We have been growing beets in our garden since we opened twelve years ago. I have also been serving Lively Run Goat cheese from Suzanne and Steve Messmer, in Interlaken, for the same length of time. We love the earthiness and the sweetness of this dish. The goat cheese mousse adds a richness and a bit of elegance to the beets. In the summer, we serve this dish with a trio of our heirloom beets that we grow—Detroits, Chiogga and Golden beets. It is topped with our micro beet greens that we grow as well.

Serves 6

ROASTING BEETS

YIELD: 6 medium-sized beets

INGREDIENTS

6 medium-sized beets (we use a combination of Detroit Red and Touchstone Gold beets from our garden)
$\frac{1}{4}$–$\frac{1}{2}$ cup water, depending on size of beets
4 sprigs fresh thyme
$\frac{1}{2}$ shallot, thinly sliced
salt and black pepper
extra-virgin olive oil

PROCESS

1. Preheat oven to 375 degrees.
2. Wash the beets under cold water and then cut off the tops and bottoms.
3. Place the beets in a shallow roasting pan.
4. Add the water, thyme springs and sliced shallots over the beets. Season with salt and pepper and then drizzle with extra-virgin olive oil.
5. Cover the pan tightly with aluminum foil and place in oven. Check the beets often to ensure the water level doesn't dissipate to the point of burning the pan.
6. To test for doneness, insert a thinly bladed knife halfway into the beet—there should not be any resistance.
7. Remove beets from the pan and leave at room temperature until cool. Once cooled, remove the skin by rubbing a paper towel against the beet.

LIVELY RUN CHÈVRE FILLING

YIELD: 1 pint or 6 assembled towers

INGREDIENTS

1 pound Lively Run Chèvre (soft goat cheese)
½ cup heavy cream, or until desired consistency
¼ cup chopped chives
salt and pepper to taste

PROCESS

1. Combine all ingredients in a mixer fitted with a paddle attachment and beat until light and fluffy.
2. If assembling towers immediately, place in piping bag fitted with a small round tip. If not, store until needed. It can be refrigerated for up to 1½ weeks.

SHERRY VINAIGRETTE

YIELD: 1 quart

INGREDIENTS

¾ cup sherry vinegar
1 shallot, finely diced
1 teaspoon kosher salt
¼ cup lemon juice
2 teaspoons Dijon mustard

2 tablespoons honey, plus more to taste
1½ cup olive oil
1½ cup grape-seed oil
Freshly ground black pepper and salt to taste

PROCESS

1. Combine the sherry vinegar, diced shallots and 1 teaspoon of kosher salt in a small bowl. Allow it to macerate for 15 minutes.
2. In blender, combine the sherry vinegar/shallot mixture, lemon juice, Dijon mustard and 2 tablespoons of honey.
3. Blend until smooth.
4. Once smooth, add olive oil and blend until incorporated.

5. Pour mixture into large bowl and whisk in the grape-seed oil by hand. Season with salt and pepper.

6. If the mixture is too acidic or tastes distinctly of vinegar, add 1–2 more tablespoons of honey to taste.

BEET ASSEMBLY

Using desired-sized circular cutter, cut the whole beet into a cylinder. Slice the beets horizontally ¼ inch thick. Place one slice of beet into ring mold and pipe a thin layer of the goat cheese mixture into the top of the beet. Repeat with another beet slice. Place the final beet slice on top of the goat cheese mixture. Remove from ring mold. Toss micro-greens in some sherry vinaigrette and place on top of the beet tower. Drizzle vinaigrette around the plate and season tower with fleur de sel. Serve with toasted walnuts and orange segments.

AUTUMN HARVEST PORK LOIN WITH CAYUGA PURE ORGANIC PINTO BEANS, ZUCCHINI, SQUASH AND LIMA BEANS
(paired with Damiani Wine Cellars Lemberger)

Suzanne and Bob love the way a medium-bodied Finger Lakes Lemberger pairs with this pork dish, so I selected Damiani Wine Cellars' version to make the recipe shine. Damiani is owned by three friends—Phil Davis, Lou Damiani and Glenn Allen—whose main mission is to show the world that beautiful red wines can be grown and crafted in the Finger Lakes. They have done just that, producing some of the highest awarded reds in the region. The Damiani Lemberger is a combination of bright red fruit and earthy tones with flavors that show off its prime vineyard location along the southeast Seneca Lake "Banana Belt." The pork in the entrée softens the acids and tannins in the wine so that the herbs and savory flavors are accentuated. The perfect bite exists when ensuring that your fork contains all the elements: pork, corn, zucchini and some beans. Make sure that you include some of the fresh rosemary in your bite as the wine extends its flavor beautifully in the finish.

Here are Suzanne's reflections on her selection:

Suzanne Fine Regional Cuisine Autumn Harvest Pork Loin with Cayuga Pure Organics Pinto Beans, Zucchini, Squash and Lima Beans paired with Damiani Wine Cellars Lemberger. *Photo by Robyn Wishna.*

I have been a fan of the heritage breed of pork that Tim and Sara Hawes offer at Autumn Harvest Farm in Romulus. The tenderloin is a lovely piece of meat to grill in the summer. Finishing the dish with a medley of summer vegetables from our garden along with our fresh herbs is a nice, light summer entrée.

Serves 6

INGREDIENTS

½ cup olive oil
¼ cup fresh lemon juice
½ teaspoon curry powder
3 cloves garlic, thinly sliced

1 1-inch piece ginger, thinly sliced
1 sprig each fresh thyme and rosemary
2 pork tenderloins

PROCESS

1. In a bowl, whisk together the oil, lemon juice and curry powder. Add the sliced garlic, ginger and fresh herbs.
2. Add the tenderloin and turn to coat—marinate for 1 hour at room temperature.
3. Remove pork from marinade and season with salt and pepper.
4. Pork can be either grilled or roasted.

TO GRILL

Grill the pork tenderloin turning occasionally for about 10 minutes. Transfer pork to a cutting board and let rest for another 10 minutes before slicing.

TO ROAST

Heat oven to 375 degrees. Sear the pork in a sauté pan until lightly caramelized. Finish the pork in the oven on a rack for about 14–18 minutes.

TO SERVE

Cut the pork into thin slices. Spoon bean mixture onto plates and drizzle with basil oil. Top with the sliced pork and a sprig of fresh rosemary and season with fleur de sel.

SUMMER VEGETABLE MEDLEY

INGREDIENTS

2 tablespoons olive oil
1 onion, finely diced
1 clove garlic, minced
1 medium zucchini, diced
1 medium squash, diced
1½ cups cooked pinto beans
½ cup lima beans

3 cups vegetable broth
1½ cups fresh corn off the cob
1 tablespoon garlic puree
2 tablespoon unsalted butter
1 cup cherry tomato halves
2 tablespoon fresh parsley and basil

PROCESS

1. Heat olive oil in a large sauté pan. Add the onion and cook, stirring until the onions have softened. This should take about 6–8 minutes.

2. Add the minced garlic and continue to cook for 1 minute.

3. Add the zucchini, squash, pinto beans and lima beans. Pour just enough vegetable broth over the mixture to cover. Season the mixture with salt and pepper and bring to a simmer. Add the corn after it has been sautéed in a bit of unsalted butter.

4. Add the garlic puree, butter and parsley. Season the vegetables again with salt and pepper. Fold in the cherry tomato halves and fresh herbs.

PEACH MELBA
(paired with King Ferry Treleaven Eis)

Peaches macerated in Treleaven Eis wine served over raspberry sauce with fresh raspberries, vanilla ice cream, toasted sliced almonds and a lavender-infused sugar cookie. Garnished with fresh lavender.

When I mentioned to Suzanne and Bob that I wanted to feature King Ferry Winery's Treleaven Eis with her dessert, she took the pairing to the next level by including it in the recipe! King Ferry Winery, located on the eastern shore of Seneca Lake, is known for its vibrant Chardonnays and Rieslings. The Treleaven Eis is an ice-styled dessert wine that is made by pressing frozen Riesling grapes to concentrate the natural sugars. The result is wine that is sweet yet balanced with a crisp acidic finish. When it is paired with Suzanne's Peach Melba, you first experience an explosion of peach flavor that continues into the finish and is highlighted by a hint of roasted almonds. The creaminess of the ice cream mixed with the macerated peaches enhances the delicate flavors of the wine, and the acidity in the wine cuts beautifully into the whole dessert, accentuating the delicate flavors of lavender and almond. It is a perfect marriage of heavenly flavors! On a side note: a bite of Suzanne's lavender shortbread cookie on its own with a sip of the wine is a love affair with butter, and the utter flakiness of this cookie is so perfect that it breaks apart in your mouth before you even begin chewing.

Here are Suzanne's thoughts on the significance behind her choice of this refreshing dessert and her commitment to garden-fresh flavors:

Our property was once a peach orchard owned by John C. Townsend, who was the original owner. In honor of Mr. Townsend, we serve this

Suzanne creates her own vanilla ice cream and lavender-infused sugar cookie for this luscious Peach Melba dessert paired with King Ferry Winery Treleaven Eis. *Photo by Robyn Wishna.*

dessert every August, when peaches are in season. We make our own ice cream and prepare a fresh lavender sugar to make lavender sugar cookies to serve with it. The lavender is grown on our property as well. We also have our own raspberry bushes on our property that we use for this dessert.

Serves 6

INGREDIENTS

1 quart vanilla bean ice cream
1 pint fresh raspberries
lavender or vanilla sugar cookies

MACERATED PEACHES

4 ripe peaches
King Ferry Treleaven Eis wine

PROCESS

1. Peel and split the peaches in half. Slice peaches about ¼ inch thick and place them in a container. Pour wine over the peaches to completely cover. Macerate for at least 4 hours.

RASPBERRY SAUCE

YIELD: 1 quart

INGREDIENTS

1 pound frozen raspberries
1 cup confectioners' sugar
1 tablespoon lemon juice or more to taste

PROCESS

1. Defrost the frozen raspberries and puree berries in a blender or with an immersion blender. Strain using a fine-mesh sieve.
2. Whisk in the confectioners' sugar and lemon juice. Taste and adjust.
3. Pour sauce in a small saucepan and place over low heat to barely simmering. Reduce sauce until it thickens slightly, approximately 30 minutes.

PEACH MELBA ASSEMBLY
(We also serve this dessert topped with fresh whipped cream)

Squirt 1 teaspoon of raspberry sauce in the bottom of the dish (we serve it in a martini glass). Place the macerated peaches on top of the raspberry sauce. Place fresh raspberries on top of the peaches, leaving a space in the middle for ice cream. Place one scoop of vanilla ice cream in the center and sprinkle toasted sliced almonds. Serve with one to two lavender sugar cookies.

SWEET ENDING

Every happy story should have a sweet ending. This is mine. Meet Emma Frisch. Some of you might already know her. Emma was a finalist on the *Food Network Star*, representing our region and all it stands for. She has a fabulous blog called Frisch Kitchen (www.emmafrisch.com) that joyously shares recipes with ingredients that "tell a story about land and culture." She is an experienced farmer and a self-taught chef. She has an infectious personality that draws people in to share in her excitement of the region. To me, she represents the next generation of Finger Lakes culinary storytellers, who appreciate and enjoy the bounty given to us and then turn it into something worth talking about.

I asked Emma to create an after-dinner chocolate bite to pair with Ports of New York's Red Meleau. Here is what Emma has to say about her Fig and Pecan Truffles:

> *I love to make bite-sized desserts—and every bite counts! For me, a recipe rarely starts from scratch, but from stories. These truffles remind me of the fig tree in my mamma's backyard, which seduces me every summer with sun-kissed fruit. I like to use Fair Trade chocolate when possible to honor the hard work of family farmers, who feed our sweet addiction with eco-friendly practices. As local-global communities become more connected, I find every bite more fulfilling when I can celebrate its roots.*

The wine served with these truffles is Red Meleau, the creation of Frédéric Bouché, owner and sole proprietor of Ports of New York in the city of Ithaca. Frédéric is a fourth-generation winemaker from Normandy, France, and makes his elegant port-styled wines with grapes from Seneca Lake and grape spirits from local distillers. As Emma and I sat in a local park sampling the red port with her truffles, we commented first on how awesome it was that our business lunch involved tasting local wine and chocolate in the park. Our second reaction was our excitement with the pairing. On its own, the port-styled red wine made from Cabernet Franc and Merlot grapes has a freshness and fruitiness to it—a remarkable lightness for a fortified wine that makes it very adaptable to many different kinds of food. But when we paired it with Emma's truffle, the wine took on a more traditional port flavor. The figs and pecans in the truffle combined with the wine to create a rich chocolate, dried fruit and nut experience that truly was the perfect ending to a great meal.

Emma Frisch literally whips up the chocolate base for the truffles in her recipe. Emma's blog, Frisch Kitchen, is filled with videos, recipes and stories that celebrate her farm-fresh approach to cooking. *Photo by Andrew Noyes*.

Emma's Fig and Pecan Truffles paired with Ports of New York Red Meleau is the perfect ending to any occasion. *Photo by Andrew Noyes.*

FIG & PECAN TRUFFLES
(paired with Ports of New York Red Meleau)

Yields 24 truffles

ACTIVE COOKING TIME: 20 minutes
INACTIVE COOKING TIME: 60 minutes

INGREDIENTS

½ pound dried black mission figs
8 ounces bittersweet chocolate chips
2 tablespoons water
2 tablespoons butter
¾ cup heavy cream
I cup whole pecans
⅓ cup cocoa powder

PROCESS

1. Prepare the figs. Remove the stems and mince the figs as best as you can—don't forget to nibble as you go.
2. In a small saucepan over low heat, add the chocolate chips and water. Stir until smooth.
3. Stir in the butter until the melted chocolate becomes smoother and shiny.
4. Drizzle in the heavy cream, stirring to mix thoroughly. Remove from heat.
5. Stir in the fig pieces and then pour the chocolate into a deep baking dish. Set in the fridge for 1 hour to harden. (Lick the pot clean.)
6. While the chocolate is setting, prepare the cocoa and pecan coating. Preheat the oven to 250 degrees.
7. Grind the pecans into a fine meal in a food processor or blender. Spread evenly on a baking sheet and toast for 10 minutes.
8. Transfer the ground pecans to a plate and toss with the cocoa powder.
9. Remove the chocolate from the refrigerator. Using your hands (our best utensils!), roll the chocolate into small balls and roll in the pecan and cocoa mixture.
10. Serve immediately or store in the refrigerator.

RECIPES AND WINE PAIRINGS

Autumn Harvest Pork Loin with Cayuga Pure Organic Pinto Beans, Zucchini, Squash and Lima Beans paired with Damiani Wine Cellars Lemberger (page 130)

Autumn Salad Plate paired with Long Point Winery Estate Chardonnay (page 100)

Beet Tower paired with Silver Thread Vineyard Gewurtztraminer (page 127)

Caramel Ginger Pumpkin Pie paired with Great Western Extra Dry Champagne (page 63)

Fig & Pecan Truffles paired with Ports of New York Red Meleau (page 138)

Fruit Cup paired with Hosmer Winery Brut Sparkling Wine (page 58)

Greek Lemon-Mint Beans and Vegetables paired with Dr. Konstantin Frank Vinifera Wine Cellars Old Vine Pinot Noir (page 103)

Meatloaf Wellington paired with Standing Stone Smokehouse Red (page 75)

Old-Fashioned Savory Apple Dumplings paired with Bet the Farm Village White (page 43)

Peach Melba paired with King Ferry Treleaven Eis (page 133)

Plum Sage Martini made with Finger Lakes Distilling McKenzie Distiller's Reserve (page 89)

Roast Turkey Breast with Half-Baked Mashed Potatoes, Squash in the Shell, Johnnycakes, Jam and Pickles paired with Hosmer Winery Pinot Noir Brut Rosé (page 58)

Rumake paired with Six Mile Creek Winery Vignoles (page 86)

Sara's Fresh Apple-Spice Cake paired with Red Newt Cellars Lahoma Vineyards Riesling (page 106)

Slow-Ass Spiced and Spiked Apple Gingerbread paired with Sheldrake Point Late Harvest Riesling (page 44)

Three Sisters Soup paired with Cayuga Ridge Chardonnay (page 31)

BIBLIOGRAPHY

Author unknown. Article in the local Ithaca paper about Ithaca and its notoriety for immorality. Date of publication unknown. http://freepages. history.rootsweb.ancestry.com/~townofithaca/maps/1866atlas/_P9D9571small.jpg.

Barber, Nelson, Lyndsey Hutchins and Tim Dodd. "A History of the American Wine Industry." Lubbock: Texas Tech University College of Human Sciences, 2007.

Bilow, Rochelle. "In the Chef's Corner with Brud Holland, Executive Chef at the Red Newt Cellars Winery and Bistro." Finger Lakes Wine Country. http://www.fingerlakeswinecountryblog.com/2012_05_01_archive.html.

Carnegie Museum of Natural History. "The Three Sisters: Sustainers of Life." http://www.carnegiemnh.org/online/indians/iroquois/sisters.html.

Cassiola, Jessie. "The Short Order: Chef Scott Signori's Guide to the Finger Lakes." http://www.gq.com/food-travel/restaurants-and-bars/201205/chef-scott-signori-scoots-finger-lakes-guide-short-order.

Cattell, Hudson. *Wines of Eastern North America: From Prohibition to Present.* Ithaca, NY: Cornell University Press, 2013.

Cornell University Library. "Cornell Bulletin for Homemakers Archive, 1901–1950." Home Economics Archive Research Tradition History. http://hearth.library.cornell.edu/h/hearth/browse/title/4732784.html.

Cornell University Library Division of Rare and Manuscripts Collections. "Song of the Vine: A History of Wine." http://rmc.library.cornell.edu/ewga.

————. "What Was Home Economics?" http://rmc.library.cornell.edu/homeEc/masterlabel.html.

Covington, Linnea. "8 Must-Visit Farmer's Markets Around the U.S." http://www.zagat.com/b/8-must-visit-farmers-markets-around-the-u.s.

Cox, Gary A. "How It Began—The Roots of Finger Lakes Wine." *Life in the Finger Lakes* (Summer 2011).

————. "A Taste of Our History." *Life in the Finger Lakes* (Summer 2012).

Crews, Ed. "Drinking in Colonial America: Rattle-Skull, Stonewall, Bogus, Blackstrap, Bombo, Mimbo, Whistle Belly, Syllabub, Sling, Toddy, and Flip." *Journal of Colonial Williamsburg Foundation* (2007).

Dawson, Evan. *Summer in a Glass: The Coming of Age of Winemaking in the Finger Lakes*. New York: Sterling Publishing, 2011.

Dr. Konstantin Frank Wine Cellars. *An American and His Wine: A Dr. Konstantin Frank Documentary*. Originally produced by Ent-Gate Films, Buffalo, New York, 1976. Digitally remastered by Media Transfer Service, Rochester, New York, 2012.

Dumas, Fran. "Way Back When in Yates County: Yates Was Fruit Basket Capital." *Finger Lakes Times*, September 30, 2012.

Edible Finger Lakes. "Finger Lakes U-Pick Farms." www.ediblefingerlakes.com/u-pick-farms.

Einset, John, and W.B. Robinson. "Cayuga White: The First of a Finger Lakes Series of Wine Grapes for New York." *New York's Food and Life Sciences Bulletin* 22 (August 1972).

Ellensburg Daily Record. "5,000 Enjoy 28-Foot Pancake." September 28, 1987.

Erie Canal Museum. "A Brief History of the Erie Canal." http://eriecanalmuseum.org/history/.

Erie Canalway National Heritage Corridor. http://www.eriecanalway.org/.

Figiel, Richard. *Culture in a Glass: Reflections on the Rich Heritage of Finger Lakes Wine*. Lodi, NY: Silver Thread Books, 1995.

Finch, Roy G. *The Story of the New York State Canals: Historical and Commercial Information*. New York State Engineer and Surveyor, 1925. Republished by New York State Canal Corporation, 1998. http://www.canals.ny.gov/history/finch_history.pdf.

Finger Lakes Museum. "Walk Through Time." http://fingerlakesmuseum.org/finger-lakes/pathways-a-map-to-the-finger-lakes/walk-through-time/.

Fortune. "Can Wine Become an American Habit?" February 1934. Republished in March 2012 at http://features.blogs.fortune.cnn.com/2012/03/25/american-wine-fortune-1934/.

Gladwin, F.E. *A History of Grape Growing in the Eastern United States*. New York: Rural Publishing Company, 1931.

Haine, Peggy. "Brown Hound Bistro." *Edible Finger Lakes: The Wine Issue* (May/June 2014).

Helper, Caroline. "New York's Finger Lakes: The Next Great Wine Region in America?" http://www.theatlantic.com/health/archive/2012/04/new-yorks-finger-lakes-the-next-great-wine-region-in-america/255037/.

Hendrick, Ulysses P. *A History of Agriculture in the State of New York*. Albany: New York State Agricultural Society, 1933.

Huffsmith, H.H. "A Descriptive Study of the Premium Finger Lakes Wine Industry in New York State." Master's thesis, Cornell University, 1973.

Iroquois White Corn Project. http://www.ganondagan.org/iwcp/about.

Jefferson, Thomas. *The Writings of Thomas Jefferson*. Edited by H.A. Washington. New York: H.W. Derby, 1861.

Marvel, Tom. "Wines of the Finger Lakes." *Gourmet* (October 1957).

Milliken, Charles, F. *A History of Ontario County, New York, and Its People*. Vol. 1. New York: Lewis Historical Publishing Co., 1911.

Molesworth, James. "Finger Lakes Forges Ahead: Riesling Makes Its Mark in This New York Wine Region." *Wine Spectator* (January–February 2013).

———. "Stirring the Lees with James Molesworth: Why Doesn't Eating Local Translate to Drinking Local?" *Wine Spectator* (June 2011).

Montana, Rob. "Sharing the Crop: Farm-to-Home Network Links Region's Consumers to Fresh Local Food." *Ithaca Journal* (April 2014).

Moosewood Collective. "About Moosewood." http://www.moosewoodcooks.com/about/.

Mt. Pleasant, Jane. *First Peoples, First Crops: Iroquois Agriculture, Past and Present*. Parts 1–5. Cornell University Cornellcast. http://www.cornell.edu/video/playlist/first-peoples-first-crops-iroquois-agriculture-past-and-present.

National Park Service. "Lamoka." http://tps.cr.nps.gov/nhl/detail.cfm?ResourceId=413&ResourceType=Site.

Nearing, Helen, and Scott Nearing. *The Maple Sugar Book*. Revised ed. New York: Schocken Books, 1971.

Near, Irwin W. *A History of Steuben County, New York, and Its People*. Vol. 1. New York: Lewis Publishing Co., 1911.

New York State College of Home Economics. *Guide to the New York State College of Home Economics Records, 1875–1979*. Cornell University Library, Division of Rare and Manuscript Collections. Collection number 23-2-749. Compiled 2001.

New York State Comptroller's Office. *The Role of Agriculture in the New York State Economy*. http://www.osc.state.ny.us/reports/other/agriculture21-2010.pdf.

New York State Secretary's Office. *Journals of the Military Expedition of Major General John Sullivan Against the Six Nations of Indians in 1779.* Auburn, NY: Knapp, Peck & Thompson, 1887.

New York Wine and Grape Foundation. "Finger Lakes Region." http://www.newyorkwines.org/Regions/FingerLakes.

———. *The New York Wine Course and Reference.* Canandaigua: New York Wine and Grape Foundation, 2013.

N.Y. ABC. LAW § 61:NY Code—Section 61: Distiller's Licenses.

Ontario County's Agricultural Adventure Trail. "Ag History." http://fingerlakesagriculture.com/AgEd/history/history.php.

Peck, Garrett. *The Prohibition Hangover: Alcohol in America from Demon Rum to Cult Cabernet.* New Brunswick, NJ: Rutgers University Press, 2009.

Pellechia, Thomas. "Bully Hill Uses Sports to Sell Wine." http://www.winesandvines.com/template.cfm?section=features&content=49806.

———. "Will Rieslings Always Reign in Finger Lakes?" *Press & Sun-Bulletin,* March 2014.

Pigott, Stuart. *Best White Wine on Earth: The Riesling Story.* New York: Stuart, Tabori & Chang, 2014.

Pinney, Thomas. *A History of Wine in America, Volume 1: From the Beginnings to Prohibition.* Berkeley: University of California Press, 1989.

———. *A History of Wine in America, Volume 2: From Prohibition to the Present.* Berkeley: University of California Press, 2005.

7 U.S. Code § 304—Investment of Proceeds of Sale of Land or Scrip. United States Code, 2006 Edition, Supplement 5, Title 7—AGRICULTURE.

Sherer, Richard. "Finger Lakes Grape Pioneers." *Vineyard View* (Autumn 1983).

Spiegelman, Robert. *Fields of Fire: The Sullivan-Clinton Campaign Then and Now.* Self-published, 2004.

Stradley, Linda. "History and Legends of Apples." http://whatscookingamerica.net/Fruit/Apples.htm.

Stringfellow, Jamie. "40 Years of Moosewood: Memories & Recipes from the Legendary Vegetarian Restaurant." http://spiritualityhealth. com/articles/40-years-moosewood-memories-recipes-legendary-vegetarian-restaurant.

Sturtevant, William, and Bruce G. Trigger. *Handbook of North American Indians, Vol. 15: Northeast.* Washington, D.C.: Smithsonian Institution, 1978.

Sumner, Daniel A., et al. *An Economic Survey of the Wine and Winegrape Industry in the United States and Canada.* Davis: University of California–Davis, 2001. http://aic.ucdavis.edu/research1/Winegrape.pdf.

Trezise, Jim. "Wine Competitions: Roads to Recognition." The WINE Press (e-mail newsletter of the New York Wine and Grape Foundation), May 2014.

26 U.S. Congress §5388. Designation of wines. United States Code, 2006 Edition, Supplement 5, Title 26—INTERNAL REVENUE CODE.

USDA National Agriculture Statistics Service. "California Grape Crush Report." March 2013.

Walter-Peterson, Hans. "A Taste of Finger Lakes History." Presentation given at the Stueben County Cornell University Cooperative Extension Annual Dinner, April 2014.

Washington, George. *The Writings of George Washington from the Original Manuscript Sources, 1745–1799.* Washington, D.C.: U.S. Government Printing Office, 1931.

Watkins Glen Chamber of Commerce. "Lamoka People." www.townoftyrone.org/Lamoka/index.html.

Wellman, Judith. *The Road to Seneca Falls: Elizabeth Cady Stanton and the First Woman's Rights Convention*. Champaign: University of Illinois Press, 2004.

Zuckerman, Jocelyn. "New York State of Mind." *Gourmet* (July 2005).

INDEX

ABOUT THE AUTHOR

Laura Winter Falk is co-owner and president of Experience! The Finger Lakes, a touring and events company in Ithaca, New York, that specializes in immersive food and wine experiences in the Finger Lakes region. She holds a PhD in nutrition and is a member of the Guild of Sommeliers. Laura's passion for wine and food started as an undergraduate at Cornell University, where she majored in nutrition and had the opportunity to take "Introduction to Wines" her senior year. Little did she know at the time that more than thirty years later, she would be living in the Finger Lakes and enjoying a career that celebrates the food and wine of the region. In addition to showing off the best that the Finger Lakes has to offer, she regularly guest lectures at Cornell University, Ithaca College and Finger Lakes Community College. Laura serves on the board of directors of the Finger Lakes Tourism Alliance and Tompkins County Chamber of Commerce and is also an appointed member of the Tompkins County Agriculture and Culinary Task Force. While she has published a number of journal articles and academic papers on food choice, healthy eating and dietary behavior change, this is her first book. Laura lives in Ithaca with her husband, Alan, and sons, Gabriel and Jackson.